THE WANDERER

OLD AND MIDDLE ENGLISH TEXTS
General Editor : G. L. BROOK

The Wanderer

Edited by
ROY F. LESLIE

MANCHESTER UNIVERSITY PRESS

Published by the University of Manchester
at THE UNIVERSITY PRESS
316–324 Oxford Road
Manchester, M13 9NR

First Published 1966
Reprinted 1969
GB SBN 7190 0120 X

Printed in Great Britain at the Aberdeen University Press

PREFACE

The Wanderer has long been regarded as one of the finest poems of the Anglo-Saxon period, although there has been no general agreement on its theme, structure or genre. In consequence the poem has attracted a considerable body of critical literature during the past century. The last twenty years have seen many notable additions which have revolutionised attitudes towards both the text and the intellectual and cultural background of the poet. It seems appropriate, therefore, to publish the first separate edition of the poem at this time. The text is based on the facsimile edition of *The Exeter Book* and has been collated with the original manuscript.

My thanks are due to the following: the Dean and Chapter of Exeter Cathedral for access to the manuscript; Professor R. M. Wilson for help and guidance; Mr. A. D. Horgan and Dr. Dorothy M. Horgan for information and advice, and for reading the typescript; Mr. E. Evans for assistance with Celtic texts; Mr. Dennis Bradley for advice on medieval Latin; Professor I. A. Richmond for information on Roman ruins in England; Professor J. C. Pope for kindly giving me access to his article on the poem in advance of publication and for reading and commenting on the introduction to this edition; Dr. R. N. Ringler for valuable suggestions and proof corrections and Miss B. M. Griffith for typing part of the book.

I owe a special debt to Dr. Ida L. Gordon for the stimulus of discussion of the poem over many years, and for reading a draft of the book and giving information and helpful criticism on many points; and to Dr. J. E. Cross, whose published work on the poem constitutes an important contribution to the study of Old English poetry, for reading the book in typescript and giving valuable advice and criticism. I am heavily indebted to Professor G. L. Brook, who has constantly made available his time and his great scholarship to the immeasurable benefit of the contents of this edition, and has given helpful advice on its form in his capacity as General Editor of the series in which it appears. My debt to my wife extends to every aspect of the preparation of this edition, from typing many versions to checking, revising and suggesting a multitude of improvements.

I should like to thank the Manchester University Press for undertaking the publication of the book, and the Secretary, Mr. T. L. Jones, for his patience and co-operation.

ROY F. LESLIE

February, 1965

CONTENTS

ABBREVIATIONS

AfdA	*Anzeiger für deutsches Altertum*
Archiv	*Archiv für das Studium der neueren Sprachen und Litteraturen*
AS	Anglo-Saxon
Beiträge	*Beiträge zur Geschichte der deutschen Sprache und Literatur*
Bessinger	J. B. Bessinger, *A Short Dictionary of Anglo-Saxon Poetry.* Toronto, 1960.
Bosworth-Toller	*An Anglo-Saxon Dictionary*, based on the manuscript collection of J. Bosworth, and edited and enlarged by T. N. Toller. Oxford, 1898.
Campbell	A. Campbell, *Old English Grammar.* Oxford, 1959.
EETS	Early English Text Society.
ELH	*English Literary History*
Gmc.	Germanic
Grein-Köhler	C. W. M. Grein, *Sprachschatz der angelsächsischen Dichter.* Revised edition by J. J. Köhler, assisted by F. Holthausen. Heidelberg, 1912.
Grein-Wülker	R. P. Wülker, *Bibliothek der angelsächsischen Poesie* I. Begründet von Christian W. M. Grein. Kassel, 1883.
Holthausen	F. Holthausen, *Altenglisches Etymologisches Wörterbuch.* Heidelberg, 1934.
JEGP, JGP	*Journal of English and Germanic Philology* (vols. i-iv under the title *Journal of Germanic Philology*).
Krapp-Dobbie	G. P. Krapp and E. V. K. Dobbie, *The Exeter Book.* New York, 1936.
L	Latin
Luick	K. Luick, *Historische Grammatik der Englischen Sprache.* Leipzig, 1921.
ME	Middle English
MLN	*Modern Language Notes*
MLQ	*Modern Language Quarterly*
MLR	*Modern Language Review*

OE	Old English
OHG	Old High German
ON	Old Norse
OS	Old Saxon
PMLA	*Publications of the Modern Language Association of America*
pp.	past participle
RES	*Review of English Studies*
Sievers-Brunner	E. Sievers, *Angelsächsische Grammatik*, revised as *Altenglische Grammatik* by K. Brunner. Second edition. Halle, 1951.
sv.	strong verb
Toller	T. N. Toller, *An Anglo-Saxon Dictionary Supplement*. Oxford, 1921.
w.	with
Wright-Wülker	T. Wright, *Anglo-Saxon and Old English Vocabularies*. Second edition edited by R. P. Wülker. London, 1884.
WS	West Saxon
wv.	weak verb
ZfdP	*Zeitschrift für deutsche Philologie*

INTRODUCTION

THE MANUSCRIPT

THE unique text of *The Wanderer* is on folios 76b-78a of *The Exeter Book*, an anthology which contains the most varied collection of the poetry which has survived from the Anglo-Saxon period. The manuscript was compiled towards the end of the tenth century and was presented to Exeter Cathedral by Leofric, the first bishop of Exeter, who died in 1072. It is still kept there in the chapter library (press mark 3501). A collotype facsimile of the manuscript was published in 1933, with a full description of its history and handwriting, by R. W. Chambers, M. Förster and R. Flower. The folios containing *The Wanderer* are completely legible and undamaged.

THEME AND STRUCTURE

The Wanderer has been a favourite anthology piece, much admired and much discussed for over a century. It is one of a group of Old English poems similar in elegiac tone and lyrical feeling. Universal in their significance, they illustrate typical human situations to which they give immediacy by portraying them through the eyes of individuals. The identity of the speaker in *The Wanderer* is of little moment, but the depth of feeling he displays preserves his individuality in the midst of the generalisations, gnomic utterances and formulaic patterns which give a wider validity to his own experiences.

Most nineteenth-century scholars believed that the poem was fundamentally a product of pagan times and were concerned to show that the Christian references in it were interpolations by monastic revisers, whose alleged contributions were deprecated. A strong reaction in support of the integrity of the text as it has been transmitted was led by W. W. Lawrence.[1] Although the interpolation theories lingered on

---

[1] For Lawrence's account of the various theories see ' *The Wanderer* and *The Seafarer* ', *JGP*, iv (1902), 460-80.

for several decades, scholars in increasing numbers accepted
the poem as it stands and controversy shifted to its theme and
structure.   There was, however, a valuable legacy from these
early   discussions: attention   was   focused   on   points   of
apparently abrupt transition of thought or mood, which called
for explanation.[1]

For some critics the narrative and elegiac parts of the poem
are the essence of the poetic inspiration and the Christian
references sops to the new religion [2]; for others the poem is a
blend of pagan and Christian elements which do not readily
coalesce.[3]   More recently discussion has been concerned with
elucidating the structural as well as the textual unity of the
poem,[4] and there is now a considerable measure of agreement
that, far from there being any inconsistency between the secular
and the religious passages, there is a deliberate juxtaposition
whose purpose is to illustrate a contrast in theme between the
transience of this world and the changelessness and security of
the heavenly kingdom.

The whole poem is not intended to be taken as the utterance of the poet in his own person, as can be seen from lines
6-7, 88-91 and 111, in which reference is made to a speaker or
speakers.   The determination of the limits of the main monologue and of the number and extent of any other speeches, has
an important bearing on any interpretation of the structure of
the poem.

[1] In a recent article, ' The Wanderer (and The Seafarer) ', *Neophilologus*, xlviii (1964), 237-51, published since this book went to press,
A. A. Prins has questioned the integrity of the transmitted text.   He
contends that the present abrupt transition in the centre of both poems
is the result of a misplacement of folios in an earlier manuscript;
restitution of the ' correct ' order of the folios would bring together the
seafaring parts of *The Wanderer* and *Resignation* into one poem.

[2] Cf. especially G. K. Anderson, *The Literature of the Anglo-Saxons*
(London, 1949), p. 159 and F. Mossé, *Manuel de l'Anglais du Moyen Âge*
(Paris, 1945), i. 403.

[3] Notably N. Kershaw, *Anglo-Saxon and Norse Poems* (Cambridge,
1922), pp. 3-5 and E. E. Wardale, *Chapters on Old English Literature*
(London, 1935), pp. 58-9.

[4] For a summary of these views see T. C. Rumble, ' From *Eardstapa*
to *Snottor on mode*: The Structural Principle of *The Wanderer* ', *MLQ*,
xix (1958), 225-30.

The wanderer's monologue has frequently been held to begin, not with the opening lines of the poem, but with line 8, because at this point the pronoun in the first person is introduced after the *swā cwæð* construction in lines 6 and 7. But a construction of this type normally has a summary or retrospective function; there is no clear evidence that it can point exclusively forward.[1] A case for the opening of the monologue at line 8 has been put forward on the basis of the similarity of lines 8 ff. to the opening lines of *The Seafarer* and *The Wife's Lament*, both of which begin with a first person formula of elegiac lament.[2] But the hardship depicted in the first five lines is similar to that in the openings of the poems cited; moreover, since there is alternation between the first and third person throughout much of what is generally accepted as the wanderer's speech, there is no reason why he should not choose to begin in the third person. On balance, therefore, there is good reason to include lines 1-5 in the monologue and to accept lines 6-7, introduced by *swā cwæð*, as parenthetical.

The first five lines consist of generalisations by the wanderer. Lines 1-2a have been held to contrast the mercy of God with the inexorability of fate, exemplified in lines 2b-5.[3] But these are not capable of being contrasted; the wanderer is maintaining that God in His mercy often chooses to override the otherwise inexorable course of events; cf. *Beowulf* 1056-7, where it is said that Grendel might well have perpetrated further wickedness *nefne him wītig God wyrd forstōde/ond ðæs mannes mōd*, and *Andreas* 459-60:

> þæt næfre forlæteð lifgende God
> eorl on eorðan, gif his ellen dēah.

It should be noted that in both passages the display of fortitude is a prerequisite of God's intervention. That a great man should possess both fortitude and wisdom is a common

[1] Cf. E. E. Ericson, *The Use of Swā in Old English* (Baltimore, 1932). Clear evidence for the use of the construction in the middle of a speech is to be found in *Christ and Satan*, 125-8.

[2] S. B. Greenfield, ' *The Wanderer*: A Reconsideration of Theme and Structure ', *JEGP*, l (1951), 456-7.

[3] Cf. B. Huppé, ' *The Wanderer*: Theme and Structure ', *JEGP*, xlii (1943), 526.

homiletic motif, whose presence in Old English poetry has been amply demonstrated by R. E. Kaske.[1] Throughout the poem the wanderer is concerned to show first how fortitude should be displayed in the face of acute personal suffering, and second how a wise man should comport himself as he contemplates human misery and the complete futility of dependence on the things of this world.

The reference in lines 2b-5 to an exile wanderer neatly summarises his own situation, which he develops and makes personal in the passage which follows. The earlier reference, to God's mercy, is not explicitly picked up again until the last lines of the poem; but the wanderer is not concerned exclusively with worldly matters in the meantime. His use of the demonstrative ' this ' with reference to ' world ' or ' life ' on no fewer than six occasions, the use of *hēr* (108-9) and of *woruldrīce* (65),[2] all show that throughout he is implying the existence of an eternal world which, as the closing lines show, is contrasted with this earthly one. A similar technique is employed in the celebrated opening description of the Earthly Paradise in *The Phoenix*.

When the poet in his own voice interrupts the monologue at lines 6 and 7, it is with one precise object in view: to emphasise the wanderer's experience, to point out that the latter has suffered the worst that life can visit upon him in the society to which he belongs and is, therefore, well qualified to speak authoritatively on the feelings and philosophy of an outcast.

The wanderer's monologue is resumed on a more personal note, recounting in lines 8-9a his own former friendless state. It is important to note the use of the past tense here; the wanderer no longer ' stands in the midst of sorrow ' as has been claimed.[3] It is the failure to recognise that the wanderer's troubles are over and done with which weakens Elliott's

[1] '*Sapientia et Fortitudo* as the controlling Theme of *Beowulf*', *Studies in Philology*, lv (1958), 423-56.

[2] This compound indicates the kingdom of this world, as opposed to the kingdom of heaven, in its frequent occurrences in OE religious poetry; e.g. eight times in *Genesis*, twice each in *Exodus* and *Elene*, and once in *Christ* and *Juliana*.

[3] Cf. Huppé, *loc. cit.* p. 535.

claim that we have to deal with a particular history rather than a personal but typical fate in the lament of the wanderer.[1] He believes that the wanderer has a guilty secret which he dare not acknowledge to anyone. Although this interpretation seems to find support in the verb *durre* ' dare ' (10), it overlooks the force of *nū* (9). There is no longer anyone left alive to whom he dare speak openly because he has outlived his friends, the men of his own generation; cf. lines 7, 31. He has become a wise man with a good share of years in the world, and he must follow the code of behaviour of such. Elliott's supposition that he dare not speak because of the guilt he hides would be more cogent if he were surrounded by his own friends, which he is not. He makes clear why he dare not speak his mind. In lines 11-14 he alludes to the custom of keeping one's thoughts to oneself, because fortitude is one virtue that will be expected of him now. To do this does not come easily to him, as is indicated by the phrasing of lines 11b-12, which imply that he knows something to his cost: cf. the similar phrasing in *Juliana* 546b-549:

> Hwæt, þū mec þrēades
> þurh sārslege; ic tō sōþe wāt
> þæt ic ǣr ne sīð ǣnig ne mētte
> in woruldrīce wīf þē gelīc.

Lines 15 and 16 have the appearance of a piece of gnomic wisdom, but Miss Williams has observed that the thought expressed is to be found nowhere else in passages or poems of gnomic verse in Anglo-Saxon literature.[2] Elliott sees in the fact that they do not constitute a stereotyped expression an indication that they arise out of a real situation [3]; but it has recently been pointed out that, though the idea of defying fate may be foreign to the Germanic peoples, it is to be found in Boethius, and in a particularly apposite form in Book 4, Prose 7 [4]; cf. the Old English translation: *Ac ǣlc mon scyle āwinnan*

---

[1] R. W. V. Elliott, ' The Wanderer's Conscience ', *English Studies*, xxxix (1958), 195.

[2] *Gnomic Poetry in Anglo-Saxon* (New York, 1914), p. 47.

[3] *loc. cit.* p. 194.

[4] W. Erzgräber, ' *Der Wanderer*: Eine Interpretation von Aufbau und Gehalt ', *Festschrift zum 75. Geburtstag von Theodor Spira* (Heidelberg, 1961), p. 61.

ǣgþer ge wiþ þā rēþan wyrde ge wiþ ðā winsuman.   Because a
sad and disturbed spirit is of no avail in resisting fate, the
wanderer goes on in lines 17-18 to point out that men desirous
of a high reputation generally keep their sorrows to themselves.
Commonly regarded as Germanic and heroic, this concept may
also owe much to classical and Christian precepts; both St.
John Chrysostom and St. Ambrose in consolatory sermons
advise that a man should endure his grief in silence and not
publish it by outward show.[1]

In lines 19-29a the wanderer makes specific application of
this reflection to his own past and gives us more information
about his own life, indicating that his troubles began with the
burial of his lord (22-3), which precipitated his departure from
his native land (20b) and his voyage across the sea to seek
another lord in whose service he could find security (25-29a).
Here ends the personal history of the wanderer.   His time of
wandering was turbulent; cf. *oft . . . mīne ceare cwīþan* (8-9)
and *oft earmcearig* (20).   Insufficient attention has been paid
to *geāra iū* in line 22.   These emphatic adverbs make clear that
all these things happened a long time ago, and underline his
present ripeness in years and experience.   In the following
lines the use of stereotyped exile-wanderer imagery suggests
that his fate is shared by many.[2]   We do not know whether
his quest was successful, whether he found a new temporal lord,
but he suggests that he found peace under God's protection.
He sought a ' giver of treasure ' (25), one who could comfort
him (28);   Cross points out that *frēfran* can mean ' console ' as
well as ' comfort ',[3] and the importance he attaches to it in his
thesis that the poem belongs to the genre of *consolatio* would
appear to be borne out in the closing lines of the poem, in
which the wanderer echoes this quest for consolation by saying
that it is good for a man to seek consolation from God, *frōfre tō
fæder on heofonum* (115a), for with Him alone is there security
(115b).

Since the use of the first person is interrupted at the end of

[1] J. E. Cross, ' On the Genre of *The Wanderer* ', *Neophilologus*, xlv
(1961), 66.

[2] S. B. Greenfield, ' The Formulaic Expression of the Theme of
" Exile " in Anglo-Saxon Poetry ', *Speculum*, xxx (1955), 205-6.

[3] *loc. cit.* p. 66.

this passage (29), the wanderer's monologue has sometimes been closed at this point.[1] But although the poem goes on to describe in the third person the hardships of a lonely man, the first person is resumed at line 58 for four and a half lines which lament the passing of kinsmen and are thus connected through identity of content, as well as identity of grammatical person, with lines 8-29a.[2] Moreover, the tendency to generalise personal experience in an impersonal form is characteristic of Old English poetry, as is the use of the *þām þe* formula to characterise such generalisations in lines 31 and 56.[3]

Although the case for ending the monologue here is not a strong one, the middle of line 29 does mark a change of tone. The central issue of the poem to this point is the personal experience of the wanderer, cast in elegiac form and referred to in the past tense; but the pattern has been varied by the alternation of individual experience and behaviour with general truths, referred to in the present tense. These generalisations are unlike those which follow line 29a in being closely related to the wanderer's own feelings and called forth by his own circumstances.

In the long passage in the third person (29b-57), the appeal is to the experience of all lonely voyagers. The *winelēas guma* (45) represents the type, of which the *eardstapa*, the wanderer himself, is an individual member. Since the passage generalises the sorrow of the outcast it is in the present tense, as such philosophical passages generally are in Old English poetry; for the same reason it contains the common generalising phrases with *sē þe* and *þām þe* formulas.[4] There appears to be little justification for beginning a new section with line 37.[5] The generalising present tense and third person begin at line

[1] By Flom, Miss Kershaw, Mossé and Krapp-Dobbie in the introduction of their edition of *The Exeter Book* (New York, 1936), p. xxxix, but not marked in their text.

[2] Cf. Huppé, *loc. cit.* p. 520.

[3] Cf. the use of this formula in an impersonal passage of the same type in *The Seafarer* 51, and at the intense climax of *The Wife's Lament* 52-3.

[4] Cf. *Guthlac* 1348-56, *The Wife's Lament* 42-53, *The Seafarer* 39-57, and *Vainglory* 67-77.

[5] As proposed by Krapp-Dobbie, *op. cit.* p. 135, and Erzgräber, *loc. cit.* pp. 63-4.

29b and continue through to line 57. The *wāt sē þe* formula
first introduced in line 29b is repeated in line 37; the *þām þe*
formula which first appears in line 31 is repeated in line 56.
Moreover, when we examine the subject matter, lines 29b-33
are seen to be a general introduction to a single topic, the
evocation of the past by the lonely voyager; there are three
sub-sections corresponding to three kinds of evocation, the
first of which is introduced at line 34, the second at line 37
and the third at line 50b.

The wanderer opens the passage by describing the state of
mind of all solitary travellers (29b-33), emphasising from
personal experience how bitter a companion sorrow can be
(29b-30) to one who is entirely alone; the characteristic litotes
of line 31 underlines this utter loneliness. He voices their
plight in lines 32-3 with a dramatic juxtaposition of the happy
past and the doleful present, such as we find as a major theme
in *The Riming Poem* and in *The Seafarer* 20-2. He then
proceeds to illustrate the psychological phenomena which
overtake the solitary one when mind and spirit are taxed by
sorrow. His experience is clearly of three kinds, each involving the resurrection of the past in a different form, each
more intense and less subject to his control than the one which
precedes it: memory, dream, and hallucination.

The realisation of what he lacks, *wunden gold* [1] and *foldan
blǣd* (32-3), leads naturally to remembrance of former happy
days. Memory recalls, not particular occasions, but the habitual
pleasures of his environment, the ministrations of servants, the
giving of treasure, the patronage of his lord at the feast (34-6);
then he recalls that all this joy has vanished—*wyn eal gedrēas.*

When he falls asleep exhausted (39-40), deprivation of his
lord's company causes him to dream (41a) that he is enacting
the ceremony of paying homage to his lord. [2] In memory he
dwelt passively on past pleasures, but in the dream he partici-
pates in a key ceremony in all its detail. He awakens to a
stark reality (45-8); seabirds preening replace his enthroned
lord, falling rime and snow replace the walls of the hall.

The keen disappointment of his return to the lonely, harsh

---

[1] As Cross points out (*loc. cit.* p. 66) *wunden gold* is a metonymy for
the generosity of a lord.   [2] See Notes to lines 41b-44.

present has made his heartache the heavier with longing for his beloved prince (49-50a); so the scene is set for the third and most powerful evocation of the past, hallucination. The wanderer makes clear that his solitary man is aware that he is dreaming by the phrase *pinceð him on mōde*, and then tells us specifically of his awakening (45). What happens next is beyond the solitary man's control and understanding. A key phrase for the lines that follow is *Sorg bið genīwad* (50); but the force of this observation is obscured by the punctuation of Krapp-Dobbie, who place stops after *geseldan* and *on weg* (53). Since the images which rise up before him in lines 51-3 are those of friends, it cannot be that their appearance causes him sorrow; his distress arises from the fact that they are mirages (54-5). That we have to do with hallucination and not voluntary recollection is made clear by comparison of line 34 with line 51. In the former it is *hē* who *gemon* ' remembers '; in the latter it is the remembrance itself, *gemynd*, which invades the man's imagination, as the past, unbidden, forces itself upon the lonely, unhappy man.[1] In explanation of the peculiar power of past joys over the minds of seafarers in particular, the wanderer inserts the parenthetic remark that the minds of seafarers often swim away.[2] The concept of the detachment of mind from body is repeated more explicitly in the next few lines (55b-57), and is somewhat similar to that in *The Seafarer* 58-60.

The first half of the poem has been devoted to the experience and limitations of the individual in the clutches of adverse fortune. The theme is now broadened in scope to include the whole of man's existence. Because the use of *ic* extends to the sentence ending in line 62, it has generally been assumed that the wanderer's speech goes as far as this line at least, even by Huppé, who believes that the tone of the second part of the poem is sufficiently different to justify its being given to a different speaker.[3] It is difficult, however, to separate the philosophic tone of lines 58-62 from that of the lines which follow. If there is a second major speaker, it is more credible

[1] For a detailed discussion of the syntax of this passage see Notes to lines 50-5.

[2] Unnecessary emendation of MS. *oft* to *eft* has frequently misdirected criticism of this passage.   [3] *loc. cit.* pp. 522-7.

that he should be introduced at line 58 than at line 62, as in Professor Pope's recent thesis.[1] He points out that if there are two speakers, both will naturally use the first person pronoun. Pope's major justifications for the introduction of a second speaker here are the sharp cleavage at line 58, the fact that the change comes not gradually but all at once, and the sweeping generalisation of the latter part of the poem, ' so much greater in range and abstraction than the wanderer's, and so objective, as having nothing to do with the speaker's personal losses'.

The abrupt transition can, nevertheless, be attributed to the deliberate intention of a single speaker, switching from the particular to the general for effect, and the completeness of the change has perhaps been overemphasised. The wanderer remains a serious candidate for the views expressed in the latter half of the poem, especially if he is shown to be mature enough to utter them, and if attributing them to him illuminates their complexities more adequately than placing them in the mouth of a second speaker. The wanderer has not only reached a state of comparative tranquillity, as Pope states, but is a man of mature years, for it is made clear in line 22 that he buried his lord a long time ago, *geāra iū*. If we grant him the percipience in the first five lines [2] to see the grace of God operating to counter the otherwise fixed course of events, then we may grant him the capacity to philosophise in the second half of the poem.

The state of mind of the speaker at line 58 is relevant to the significance of the latter part of the poem. It has been claimed that his mind is saddened by what he sees [3]; but he states no more than that the things of this world are calculated to make him sad. Lines 58-9 are nothing more than a rhetorical comment on what is to follow, namely the wanderer's explanation of how wisdom brings peace of mind despite loss of earthly

[1] J. C. Pope, ' Dramatic Voices in *The Wanderer* and *The Seafarer* ', *Franciplegius: Medieval and Linguistic Studies in Honor of Francis Peabody Magoun, Jr.* (New York, 1965), pp. 165-7.

[2] These lines are accepted by Pope as part of the wanderer's speech.

[3] Ida L. Gordon, ' Traditional Themes in *The Wanderer* and *The Seafarer* ' *RES* v (1954), 6, and J. E. Cross, *loc. cit.* p. 67; see also Notes to lines 58-9.

fortune.[1] He does not, in these lines, identify himself with
the ' wise man ' of lines 73-4 and 88-9, whose view is bounded
by the visible world. He has seen beyond it, as indicated in
lines 114-15, and is therefore concerned to point out the utter
instability of this world, and, at the end of the poem, to draw a
moral from it. Throughout there is implied a contrast of this
world with the kingdom of heaven, of a type familiar in Old
English homiletic literature,[2] and the use of *fæstnung* (115) to
describe heaven is but the final explicit emphasis on what has
been implicit all through the poem.

The wanderer sets the stage for his broader theme in lines
58-63; all men depart and creation daily decays. Two words,
Forþon the opening word and *eal* (60), show a connection with
the preceding part of the poem. *Forþon* as an adverb generally has a linking function, however vague, and *eal* refers to the
whole life of men, that is, not simply the experience of one
individual with which the wanderer has just been concerned.
Pope, in support of a second speaker here, suggests that the
possessive *mīn* in line 59 takes on an extra meaning which
explains why it carries the alliteration; the thinker is saying
' *my* mind also, like the wanderer's '. But we are not really
justified in taking this construction as anything more than a
stylistic device for, twice in the earlier part of the poem, in lines
10 and 19, *minne* in the second half-line alliterates with *mōdsefan*
in the first; the use of a similar construction in line 59 supplies
evidence, therefore, not for a new speaker but for continued
reference to an earlier one.

As at the outset of his personal elegy, the wanderer crystal-
lises his theme in the opening lines of his impersonal elegy.
He follows it with a bridge passage, which has troubled many
critics, before he goes on to deal with the two parts of his
general theme, first the disappearance of man and then the
disappearance of man's works and environment. The function
of lines 64-72 has generally been underestimated and their
presence condemned; but they have a significant part to play
in the poem. The clue to their interpretation lies as much in

---

[1] Cf. R. M. Lumiansky, ' The Dramatic Structure of the Old English
Wanderer ', *Neophilologus*, xxxiv (1950), 108.

[2] Cf. especially Vercelli Homily XIV.

the speaker's stress on the wisdom of the man referred to in lines 73, 88 and 90, as in the preceding lines, in which general gnomic reflections follow naturally from the speaker's observations on the mortality of men. The particular reflection in lines 61-62a prompts the general one in lines 62b-63; the connection of ideas is indicated by *swā*, for as individuals perish, so does the world.[1] One reflection continues to prompt another, and so in line 64 the speaker states the paradox whereby the passage of time, which carries all things to oblivion, including man himself, is yet a paramount requirement for gaining the cardinal asset—wisdom.[2] A somewhat different interpretation of these lines suggests that although earthly things are perishing daily, man cannot recognise the universality of this decay till the experience and reflection of many years have brought it home to him.[3] But recognition of the universality of decay is not yet a point at issue, as it becomes in the passage beginning with line 73. Whether the adverb *Forþon* (64) is taken adversatively to mean ' and yet ', or as a loose connective ' and so ', the point emphasised in the *Forþon* clause is the same—namely that wisdom comes with ripeness of experience; this wry reflection is prompted by the otherwise entirely destructive function of the passage of time indicated throughout the preceding six lines.

The continuity of thought in this passage militates against closing the wanderer's monologue at either line 62 or 63.[4] Although the use of the first person ends here, there is no sudden change from narrative to didactic verse; that change has already taken place at line 58. Huppé's argument that the contents of lines 62-87 make them incompatible with the previous lines, which are certainly in the monologue, is based

---

[1] Cf. Blickling Homily V (EETS edition), p. 59: *þes middangeard daga gehwylce fealleþ and tō ende efsteþ.*

[2] Cf. *wintrum frōd* in *Beowulf* 1724, 2114; Hroðgar's age as well as his wisdom is emphasised.

[3] S. B. Greenfield, *JEGP* 1 (1951), 458.

[4] Huppé alone has followed Klipstein in closing the monologue in the centre of line 62. The revised edition (14th) of H. Sweet's *Anglo-Saxon Reader* by C. T. Onions has quotation marks at the end of line 63. Sweet himself in earlier editions had indicated no closing point for the monologue.

on the assumption that the monologue reveals only a pagan attitude to life, and that the didacticism which follows is not consonant with it. But the use of preconceptions about the character of the monologue to determine its boundaries weakens his argument, and there are inconsistencies in his deductions about the use of the pronoun *ic* which have been clearly demonstrated in the article by Greenfield quoted above.

After discussing the prerequisite for gaining wisdom, the wanderer enumerates the elements of which it consists (65b-72), the principal stress being laid on the value of moderation. The succession of formulaic expressions consisting of *ne tō* followed by an adjective indicating a trait of human nature, is one which is found in the works of Anglo-Saxon homilists, where the sentiments expressed are often similar,[1] although those admonitions which are as much heroic as Christian, namely *ne tō wāc wiga, ne tō wanhȳdig* (67) and *ne tō forht* (68), appear to have no precise counterparts in the homilies. But there is a comparable passage in the Christian poem *Andreas*, in which there is considerable sympathy with these old heroic sentiments: *Ne bēo ðū on sefan tō forht,/ne on mōde ne murn* (98-9). That a wise man's code of moderation may have a similar expression in both pagan and Christian teaching appears from a comparison of an inscription cited by Plutarch with writings by Ambrose and Jerome, who quote the saying of the Seven Wise Men of Greece, ' nothing in excess '.[2] From an Irish source, to be dated to the early ninth century in its present form, comes a passage similar in content and form to that in *The Wanderer*. It appears in one of the gnomic collections of instructions to young aristocrats, *The Instructions of King Cormac MacAirt*:

> Be not too wise, be not too foolish,
> be not too conceited, be not too diffident,
> be not too haughty, be not too humble,

[1] See Miss Dorothy Bethurum, *The Homilies of Wulfstan* VIIIc, lines 168-71 and Xc, lines 97-100, and cf. Miss Kershaw *op. cit.* pp. 164-5, Fr. Klaeber, *JEGP*, xii (1913), 259, and Miss Elizabeth Suddaby, *MLN*, lxix (1954), 465-6. Miss Bethurum notes that the idea of the Golden Mean was not found by Wulfstan in his sources, nor was this manner of expression. [2] J. E. Cross, *loc. cit.*, p. 68.

> be not too talkative, be not too silent,
> be not too harsh, be not too feeble.[1]

The last three lines of this passage (70-2) have been described as a ' feeble expansion of line 69 '.[2] But the prominent position of the lines at the end of a passage of maxims, as well as the extent of the ' expansion ', should make us pause. Is it true that ' twice the speaker warns men against uttering boasts before they know fully how things are going to turn out '?[3] The injunction in line 69 is part of a list of exhortations to moderation that a wise man should heed; *gielpes tō georn* probably refers to the aspiration to glory, which should be kept within bounds.[4] The absolute use of the verb in the clause *ǣr hē geare cunne* indicates that it is to be taken with all the injunctions. The last three lines are, however, outside this framework. They are distinct in that they do not apply only to the wise man of line 65, but to men in general, as indicated by *beorn*, and in that they refer to a particular *bēot* ' vow ' or ' promise ',[5] stressing the necessity of being certain of what one intends before giving one's pledged word. There is a repetition of this admonition in a decidedly Christian homiletic form in line 112; but what is striking here is the phrasing of the admonition as a piece of gnomic wisdom, using *bēot* with its predominantly heroic associations. This two-fold approach to the same code of behaviour is a variant of a duality which runs through the whole passage of injunctions. None are predominantly to be associated with Christian teaching, although many are to be found in similar homiletic lists, the exceptions being those appropriate to a warrior (67-68b); and yet the form which they take is a familiar homiletic one. This calculated ambiguity is repeated several times in the latter part of *The Wanderer*, and embraces both Christian teaching in readily identifiable stereotyped forms and the noblest of the

[1] Edited and translated by Kuno Meyer, Royal Irish Academy, Todd Lecture Series XV (Dublin, 1909), p. 45.

[2] A. J. Wyatt, *An Anglo-Saxon Reader* (Cambridge, 1919), p. 264.

[3] R. W. V. Elliott, *loc. cit.* p. 195.

[4] Cf. *gilpgeorn* in the Old English translation of Bede, and the discussion of *gelp* which constitutes section X in *The Metres of Boethius*.

[5] Cf. *Beowulf* 80, 523, *The Battle of Maldon* 15, 213, and *gebēot* in *The Husband's Message* 49.

heroic virtues, as if to emphasise that the wise man postulated by the wanderer in his monologue is but a step from Christianity in his code of behaviour. Yet his philosophy is one of despair, for he lacks the ultimate salvation of the Christian, permanent security under an all-powerful Lord.

Lines 73-87 contain the first part of an impersonal elegy on the decay of the works of men, similar in style to another Old English elegiac lyric, *The Ruin*. This vivid picture of ruin gives a foretaste of what it will be like when the whole world shares the same fate (73-4). Here is the point of fusion of the themes stated in lines 63 and 65a, namely the daily decay of the world and the wisdom gained only in maturity. The man who has lived long enough to recognise the inevitability of decay is the wise man who can project his experience into the future, and who has the imagination to realise how terrible it will be when all the riches of the world stand desolate (73-4). Ambrose lists this ability as one of the prerequisites of wisdom:

> Sed etiam futurorum interpres sapientia est,
> scit praeterita, et de futuris aestimat. Scit
> versutias sermonum, et solutiones argumentorum.
> Signa et monstra scit antequam fiant, et eventus
> temporum et saeculorum.[1]

The wanderer then proceeds to exemplify and give substance to his projection in his poignant description of crumbling walls and mouldering buildings, commenting on the fate of those who had left them behind to decay. Huppé suggests that this description is a Christian reference to Doomsday, but, as has been pointed out, the tone of the passage is not exclusively Christian.[2] Early Christian writers used this theme, which they had taken over from their pagan predecessors,[3] and the reference to God in the last three lines indicates that the Last Judgment was not absent from the mind of the poet; but the emphasis on the effects of storm and rime, and later of snow and hail, are Anglo-Saxon modifications in *The Wanderer*. Even in the one explicit reference to the Christian God, the

---

[1] *Patrologia Latina*, XIV, col. 492.

[2] S. B. Greenfield, *JEGP* 1 (1951), 459.

[3] J. E. Cross, *loc. cit.* pp. 68-9.

ælda Scyppend (85), there is ambiguity; with fine irony the kenning referring to His creative activity is used in a passage describing His destructive role.

The impression that the ambiguity is deliberate is reinforced by the use the poet has made of the *sum . . . sum* formula (80-4). In an article on the incidence of the figure which includes this formula in Old English prose and poetry, Cross has shown its prevalence in Latin and Greek Christian literature to exemplify ways of bodily destruction.[1] That the poet has drawn upon this well-known Christian theme seems likely, as Cross suggests, both from the contents of the list and from the formula in which it is expressed. But it must not be forgotten that the poet has adapted the theme to his context, and that the limits he sets upon it are those appropriate to that context. The wanderer has just informed us that the buildings have crumbled and all the men have fallen by the wall (79-80). The following lines contain four successive statements introduced by forms of the indefinite pronoun *sum*. The first opens with the plural form *sume*, when the wanderer declares that war carried some off. A list of fates of men after battle in *Elene* 131-7 begins in precisely the same way, but goes on to discuss the fates of others in groups, whereas the wanderer takes up in turn the different fates of individuals in the three following phrases, each opening with *sumne*. We cannot be certain whether the use of the singular is distributive, so that each of the fates which follows refers to men struck down by war, as indicated in the *sume* phrase (80) [2] and suggested by lines 79-80a which tell how all fell in the prime of their manhood, or whether they are to be taken as fates in addition to that of men killed in battle. Whichever may be the case, the use of the singular serves to make the fates typical and hence stereotyped, as they are throughout the Old English poem *The Fortunes of Men*.

The fate of one man is to be carried off across the deep sea

[1] ' On *The Wanderer* lines 80-4: A Study of a Figure and a Theme ', *Vetenskaps-Societetens i Lund, Årsbok*, 1958-9, pp. 77-110; cf. particularly the short lament of Gregory Nazianzen which combines this figure with the *ubi sunt* motif as in *The Wanderer* (p. 94).

[2] This suggestion by Bright is supported by J. C. Pope, *loc. cit.* p. 172 and footnote 13.

by a bird. This may be a thematic bird,[1] or, as argued in the Notes, a sea-eagle, one of the ' beasts of battle '; but we do not have to decide between them, for both may well be intended. That one of the ' beasts of battle ' is intended in the fate of the second man is highly probable. Almost all the Greek and Latin Christian texts, and all the Old English homilies which deal with the ways of bodily destruction, contain a reference to death by the agency of unspecified wild animals. Specific reference to the wolf as an agent of death is made only in the Old English poetic treatments of the theme, in *The Wanderer* and in *The Fortunes of Men* 12-13. It is not enough to explain this fact simply as a desire for realism. When poets choose to depart from their sources to introduce an animal so charged with significance as the wolf, which hovers frequently, along with the carrion birds, near scenes of carnage in Old English poetry,[2] we cannot exclude symbolic intent. Here is one more example of a common theme of Christian writings being first evoked and then given an Anglo-Saxon orientation. The third man is given normal burial by a friend who has survived him; a touch of individuality is given, not to the dead, but to the man who buries him and who is described as *drēorighlēor* ' sad-faced '. We may assume from this adjective that he is emotionally involved with the deceased, who was his comrade, or perhaps his lord, and the wanderer may be remembering his burial of his own lord, described in lines 22-3; the speaker may also be touching on the elegiac motif of the last survivor, which is so movingly developed in *Beowulf* 2236-70.

The identity of the man *Sē . . . þās word ācwið* in lines 88-91 has been the subject of considerable discussion. Since a new speaker is introduced here, the end of line 87 has been suggested, though rarely adopted, as a closing point for the wanderer's monologue, and the speaker introduced at line 88 can be held to be another major character.[3] But since *þisne*

[1] Cross, ' On *The Wanderer* lines 80-84 ', p. 92.

[2] See F. P. Magoun, ' The Theme of the Beasts of Battle in Anglo-Saxon Poetry ', *Neuphilologische Mitteilungen*, lvi (1955), particularly p. 88 and footnote, also A. Bonjour, ' Beowulf and the Beasts of Battle ', *PMLA*, lxxii (1957), p. 568 (footnote), and E. G. Stanley, *Anglia*, lxxiii (1955), 442-3.

[3] See Miss Kershaw, *op. cit.* p. 3 and Huppé, *loc. cit.* pp. 519, 527.

wealsteal (88) and *þis deorce līf* (89) point back to the previous passage, and since *ācwið* (91) is in the present not the past tense as is *cwæð* in lines 6 and 111, lines 88-91 should be taken to introduce a speech within the wanderer's monologue by the ' wise man ', who is the wanderer's ' man of straw ', none other than the *glēaw hæle* of line 73, who has observed the decay portrayed in lines 75-87.[1] The devastation which he has observed gives him the subject matter for his meditations and leads him almost inevitably to generalisation and quotation of a version of the well-known *ubi sunt* formula. He is the man who ' ponders this dark life deeply ', wise by the standards of this world, whose outlook the wanderer has been discussing since line 65. The wanderer agrees with his postulated wise man, who has learned that nothing in this world is stable; but he does not restrict himself to the wise man's this-worldly wisdom. Lines 88-9 echo in part the wanderer's words in lines 58-60, but with a significant difference; whereas life is accepted as dark by the wise man in line 89 and his cry in lines 92 ff. is one of deep pessimism, the wanderer had stated that life would cause him to despair only if his observations were confined to the present world (58-60). Here is the vital distinction to be made between the wanderer and his puppet. While the latter speaks with earthly wisdom at his disposal and the apparent futility of life defeats him, the wanderer can refrain from despair because he sees the other-worldly goal which gives this life its significance. It is not, however, until he has driven home the hopelessness of a this-worldly philosophy that he lights up, briefly but positively, this desolate landscape with the certain knowledge of the world to come, which has buoyed up his own faith and enabled him so steadfastly to contemplate the suffering and ruin which he has experienced.

In lines 92 ff. we have the substance of the wise man's lament. In the light of Cross's comparative survey of the *ubi sunt* passages in Old English texts, there can be little doubt about the indebtedness of this passage to the *ubi sunt* formulas

---

[1] Cf. Lawrence, *loc. cit.* p. 474, whose first ' man of straw ' is *sē þe cunnað* (29), now generally held to be the wanderer himself, generalising his own experience.

widely current in medieval Christian homilies.[1]   There were
two major versions of the basic formula: one asked where had
gone either named heroes of antiquity or the various kinds of
potentates such as kings, princes, emperors, as in *The Seafarer*
82-5; the other version asked where had gone an often copious
variety of past splendours and joys, the objects themselves
reflecting the tastes of the period and society in which the
writer lived, from the early centuries of our era onward, and
from all over the known world from Syria to Ireland.

A close parallel to the phrasing of *The Wanderer* is to be
found in the Latin homily which begins

> Ubi ergo abierunt illa omnia?   Ubi pompa,
> ubi schemata?   Ubi exquisita convivia? [2]

The question form, the references to past splendours, the use of
abierunt in place of the more common *sunt*, all constitute
precedents for *The Wanderer*.   There is an Old English
translation of this homily, Blickling Homily VIII, which
furnishes parallels for the poet's version of the formula.   The
Latin verb *abierunt* is translated as *gewiton*, and the questions
are asked in the form *hwǣr cwōm* as well as *hwǣr byð*.[3]   The
diversity of lists of things, qualities and people whose passing
is noted in various versions of the formula provides a basis for
the compilation by the *Wanderer* poet of his own list, although
individual items may have their counterparts elsewhere.   It
should be noted that the subjects of the exclamatory part of
the passage, introduced by *Ēalā*, are of a similar type to those
in the formal questions.   As with the *sum sum* formula, the
form of the passage owes much to Latin Christian models, but
the spirit which informs it has strong heroic overtones.   Once
again the calculated ambiguity of the poet is apparent.

It has generally been assumed that the wise man's speech
continues to the close of line 110, coincident with the end of the

---

[1] ' " Ubi Sunt " Passages in Old English—Sources and Relationships ', *Vetenskaps-Societetens i Lund, Ärsbok*, 1956, pp. 25-44;   cf.
particularly pp. 39-41.

[2] *Sermones ad Fratres in Eremo* 58, in Migne's *Patrologia Latina* XL,
col. 1341; this sermon is repeated as No. 75 of the collection, with a different and shorter introduction, a clear attestation of its popularity.

[3] Cf. the *ubi sunt* passages in Blickling Homily X and Vercelli
Homily X.

wanderer's speech, of which it forms a part.[1] But the *ubi sunt* formula, which he exists to utter, ends with line 96, as can be seen from comparison of lines 95b and 96 with Isidore of Seville's famous *ubi sunt* prototype, which concludes, after the series of questions, with the following words:

> quasi umbra transierunt velut somnium evanuerunt;
> quaeruntur et non sunt.[2]

Many versions of the formula have this or a similar ' answer ' to the questions and, like the line and a half in *The Wanderer*, suggest that the objects or persons might well never have existed. *The Metres of Boethius X* deals, like the latter part of *The Wanderer*, with the conduct and outlook of the wise man; it too has a version of the *ubi sunt* formula, in which the poet asks where are the wise men of antiquity such as Brutus and Cato; like the *Wanderer* poet, he adds a Germanic note to the formula, in his case by asking where are the bones of Weland, who is unknown to the Latin text of Boethius. He ends the *ubi sunt* section:

> Hī wǣron gefyrn   forð gewitene:
> nāt nǣnig mon,   hwǣr hī nū sindon.

Since the wise man has been chosen by the poet of *The Wanderer* to utter a stereotyped form of lament, it is reasonable to suppose that his utterance closes with the end of that lament. Moreover, line 97 begins a passage in a different vein; we are back with the ruins and the vanished warriors of lines 75-80. We are also back with the present tense, which continues to line 110, broken only by two parenthetic explanatory lines (99-100); lines 92-6 are isolated by being in the past tense.

In lines 97-110 the impersonal elegy of lines 73-87 is resumed by the wanderer in his own person, but from a slightly different point of view. In the foreground now are not the fallen warriors of lines 79-84, but the wall by which they fell. His concern here is to point out how the works of man have out-lasted him; but just as man is destroyed by weapons, so his works in their turn are destroyed by the merciless elements.

---

[1] Cf. Greenfield, *loc. cit.* p. 460; Kennedy alone closes it earlier, at the end of line 96, in *Old English Elegies* (Princeton, 1936), p. 50.

[2] *Patrologia Latina* LXXXIII, col. 865.

The culmination is reached in line 110 with the statement that all the world grows waste. The line echoes, but also enlarges the scope of line 87; there the buildings stand empty of inhabitants, now they themselves are included in the general destruction.

Many have followed Grein in closing the wanderer's monologue at the end of line 110, seeing in *Swā cwæð snottor on mōde* (111a) an indication that the speech is finished.[1] Huppé has argued that line 110 closes only the speech beginning at line 92 with the *ubi sunt* formula; but the verb *ācwið* which introduces this speech is in the present tense, and is to be taken as iterative, as indicated by *feor oft gemon* in line 90. The speech to which it refers cannot, therefore, be closed by *cwæð* in line 111, which must refer to a speech begun prior to line 88, namely the wanderer's monologue.

Line 111 is, like lines 6-7, to be taken as an interpolation by the poet in his own person,[2] at a convenient point in the wanderer's speech, in which he draws attention to the fact that the reflective part of the poem, from line 62, is part of the train of thought of the wanderer, who is wise by experience. The interpolation is necessary because the wanderer has had no occasion to identify himself by the first person pronoun as he did earlier in the poem. Pope acknowledges the plausibility of the argument that ' having appeared to us at first as merely an *eardstapa*, he has earned by his discourse the epithet of a wise man, a *snottor on mōde* '. Nevertheless he sees in the difference of epithet confirmation, in the poet's own words, of his thesis that there are two different major speakers in the poem.[3] The poet's own words may, however, be held to point to a quite different conclusion. He has established the identity of his speaker by the noun *eardstapa* in line 6 and the descriptive adjectival phrase in line 111 emphasises another facet of the same man. Pope's suggestion, that *swā cwæð snottor on mōde* is a self-contained statement of the same order as *swā cwæð eardstapa*, is difficult to sustain in face of the Old English poetic practice of providing a referent, either noun or

---

[1] They include Lawrence, Kennedy and Greenfield.

[2] Cf. Lumiansky, *loc. cit.* p. 105.

[3] *loc. cit.* pp. 165-167.

pronoun, for an adjectival phrase of this kind.[1] The only possible referent here is *eardstapa*.

Another question of some importance, but difficult to answer decisively, is whether *on mōde* is to be taken with *cwæð*, to stress the inward nature of his meditations,[2] or as part of a stereotyped phrase with *snottor*, similar in kind to *frōd in ferðe* (90) or *wīs on gewitte* (*Andreas* 470). The difficulty is that there are no analogous *snottor* phrases; *mōd* is usually linked to *snottor* in the oblique cases,[3] and poets appear to prefer alliteration in phrases such as *snottor in sefan* (*Exodus* 439). Pope believes that even if we take the phrase ' as meaning primarily '' sat apart communing with himself '' it suggests that he would normally have been expected to be communing with others '. This expectation might be justified if the phrase were *tō rūne* as in the parallels he cites,[4] but here it is *æt rūne*, ' in counsel ', whereas the contexts of *tō rūne* indicate that a meaning ' in consultation ' would be the appropriate one. That the counsel the wanderer takes is inward is a possible interpretation of *on mōde*; that he is apart from others is indicated by *sundor*. This interpolated line meets the objection that the wanderer's monologue violates the noble custom that a man should keep his woes to himself (11-14).[5] We are reminded that the wanderer is in fact ' thinking as he will ' (14b).

The last four lines of the poem contain sentiments which are similar in kind to those in lines 65-72, but which have a more specifically Christian formulation and application. In lines 112-13 the wanderer once again warns against overhasty conduct, as Elliott has pointed out.[6] But whereas, in the earlier passage, reference was to the consequences of a vow, here any form of extravagant emotion indulged on impulse is

[1] Cf. *frōd in ferðe* (90) whose referent is *Sē* (88); *rǣdum snottor, wīs on gewitte* (*Andreas* 469-70), whose referent is *cempa* (461) varied by *ōreta* (463); and, after a speech, *hildedēor* (*Beowulf* 312), whose referent is *weard* (286).   [2] Cf. *þinceð him on mōde* (41).

[3] Cf. *mōde snottor* (*Riddle* 84. 35), *mōdes snottor* (*Precepts* 87) and *mōde snottre* (*Riddle* 86. 2).

[4] *Beowulf* 171-2 and *Andreas* 1161.

[5] Cf. Susie I. Tucker, ' Return to *The Wanderer* ', *Essays in Criticism*, viii (1958), 233.   [6] *loc. cit.* p. 195.

deprecated. The concept is similar to that expressed many times in the Book of Proverbs,[1] but particularly in 29.11:

> A fool gives full vent to his anger,
> but a wise man quietly holds it back.

It is not only the concept but also the manner of expression which is subtly different in this closing passage. The speaker uses formulas closely associated with homiletic writing. Line 112a has no exact counterpart, but the formula, adjective followed by *biþ sē þe*, is an established one in didactic passages in Old English poetry.[2] As has been pointed out, *til* is used in Old English of God's goodness,[3] and the adjective is associated with fidelity in *Riddle* 26, on the bible codex, in line 23, where friends are referred to as *tilra ond getrēowra*. Beside the virtue of self-control the speaker puts that of fortitude; that *ellen* can be a specifically Christian virtue is made explicit in *Andreas*:

> Forþan ic ēow tō sōðe   secgan wille,
> þæt næfre forlæteð   lifgende God
> eorl on eorðan,   gif his ellen dēah.   (458-60).

The key to the wanderer's emphasis on prudent behaviour and fortitude is his insistence throughout the poem on the failure of this world to provide consolation. The early Christian fathers had been well aware that things of this world offer no real consolation, and Cicero before them had stated that secular consolation was poor consolation.[4]

The last line and a half provide a solution to the whole problem of the transitoriness of all things, which has been posed throughout the poem. Reliable consolation is at hand if one seeks the grace of God; in *frōfre* is an echo of lines 25-9, where the wanderer as a young man sought a lord who would comfort him in his friendless state, *sōhte . . . þone þe . . . mec frēondlēasne frēfran wolde*. In form these last one and a half lines are typical

---

[1] E.g. 10. 19; 13. 3; 15. 28; 21. 23; 29. 20.

[2] E.g. *Dol biþ sē þe . . .* in *The Seafarer* 106, *Maxims I* 35, *Solomon and Saturn* 225, *Ēadig bið sē . . .* in *The Seafarer* 107, and *Bald bið sē . . .* in *Solomon and Saturn* 243.

[3] Susie I. Tucker, *loc. cit.* p. 232.

[4] Cross, ' On the Genre of *The Wanderer* ', p. 70.

of Christian exhortations not only in the prose homilies, but in poetry also, as in *The Phoenix* 516-17: *Wel biþ þām þe mōt in þā geōmran tīd Gode līcian*,[1] and *Beowulf* 183-8:

> Wā bið þǣm þe sceal
> þurh slīðne nīð sāwle bescūfan
> in fȳres fæþm, frōfre ne wēnan,
> wihte gewendan! Wēl bið þǣm þe mōt
> æfter dēaðdæge Drihten sēcean
> ond tō Fæder fæþmum freoðo wilnian!

This formula, adverb followed by *biđ þām þe*, is simply a variant of the adjectival one in line 112 already discussed. The use of *fæstnung* in the abstract sense ' stability ' [2] is unique in Old English, but when one considers the world's wealth which *wēste stondeð* (74), and the buildings which *īdlu stōdon* (87), it is not surprising that stability should be the feature of the eternal world which is stressed.

The view that the introduction and conclusion are closely unified by explicit mention of the contrast between pagan and Christian ideas ' in supplementation of each other,' [3] presents too stark an antithesis. Rather is there a contrast between the man who ignores, or is ignorant of, the world to come, and yet experiences God's grace (1b), and the man who actually seeks that mercy (114b). The virtues which are extolled in the gnomic passages are remarkable for being consistent with either a heroic or a Christian society, and those which are urged in the closing lines are the noblest of the not exclusively Christian virtues: fidelity, self-control, courage. These, of course, are not enough; the wanderer himself had demonstrated in the first fifty-seven lines of the poem that they provided neither consolation nor peace of mind. They are not the highest virtues of which man is capable under the inspiration of Christianity, such as loving one's neighbour as oneself, laying down one's life for one's brother, or turning the other cheek. The poet, however, is not concerned here with the

[1] Cf. the practically identical passage in *Christ* 1079b-1080, also *Christ and Satan* 364 and *Andreas* 885-6.

[2] Cf. Susie I. Tucker, *loc. cit.* p. 237; Erzgräber, *loc. cit.* p. 76, footnote 70; and Note to this line.

[3] S. B. Greenfield, *loc. cit.* p. 465.

specific virtues of Christianity, but rather to point out that the best of the heroic virtues are insufficient for lasting security, and that the gloom and despair which consideration of this world alone may arouse in the breast of even the wisest non-Christian, may be avoided by recognition of the fact that stability is to be found in God alone.

SOURCES AND ANALOGUES

Detailed consideration of the structure of the poem has revealed at more than one point a familiarity on the part of the poet with a Latin culture which he both echoes and adapts to his own ends. Most critics are agreed on this point, even if they differ considerably about the precise significance of the poet's Christian heritage and about the route by which he has acquired it.

An earlier, ' romantic ' view of the origins of this poem, as of the other lyrics with elegiac overtones,[1] assumes that they were basically of Germanic origin, developments either of the lyrical parts of poems like *Beowulf* or of pagan funeral laments.[2] It may be that elegiac traditions of this origin reinforced the elegiac mood in Old English poetry, particulary in the Father's Lament (*Beowulf* 2444-62); but there are so many aspects of these elegiac lyrics which are unconnected with the localised formal background of the occasional lament that it is difficult to believe that such could be the principal source of their form. The very complexity of the texture of these poems gives rise to doubts about the adequacy of vernacular origins alone and has led scholars to adduce influence from the classics, particularly from Virgil and Ovid.[3] There is, however, a wide difference of atmosphere between the Latin poets and the Anglo-Saxons, to whom the urbanity of the former is alien.

[1] These include *The Seafarer, The Wife's Lament, The Husband's Message* and *The Ruin.*

[2] Cf. R. Kögel, *Geschichte der deutschen Literatur,* I (Strassburg, 1894), 62, and L. L. Schücking, ' Das angelsächsische Totenklagelied ', *Englische Studien,* xxxix (1908), 1-13.

[3] R. Imelmann, *Forschungen zur altenglischen Poesie* (Berlin, 1920), pp. 188 ff., and H. Reuschel, ' Ovid und die ags. Elegien ', *Beiträge,* lxii (1938), 132-42.

The classics may have had some influence on their style, but they are unlikely to have been a major source of influence.

Much more promising are the writers in Latin from the fifth century onwards, mostly of Spanish, Gaulish, Irish or Anglo-Saxon origin, in whose works are combined the influence of the great patristic writers, such as Augustine, Jerome, Gregory and Ambrose, and their own native developments of Christian thought and writing. It is in the second part of *The Wanderer*, from line 58 onwards, that the clearest traces of this kind of background are to be found, as in lines 66b onwards in the similarly constructed *Seafarer*.

Clear analogues in such texts have been discussed above in respect of lines 80-4 and 92-6, and Old English homiletic ones in respect of lines 66 ff. Analogues from similar sources occur in the latter part of *The Seafarer*. In both poems the question arises whether these analogues constitute the sources from which the poets drew their materials, or whether, as Mrs. Gordon suggests, there is ' another recension, different from any yet identified, which supplied the basis for the reflections on mortality in the Old English homilies. . . . All the ideas it must have contained are to be found in popular patristic sources, chiefly those attributed in the early Middle Ages to Augustine and Isidore, and these ideas must at some stage have been assembled into a stylized pattern.'[1] However, the immense popularity between the sixth and ninth centuries of *florilegia* culled from patristic writings [2] must dispose us to grant the Old English poets the freedom to adapt and assemble for themselves matter from many sources, rather than restrict them to exemplars in which the materials they use are already combined. These *florilegia* played an important part in monastic education. Although compilers might well draw a sequence of related ideas from the same source, and they could be relied upon to excerpt from the standard collections, they often ranged very widely. Among the most celebrated collections were Isidore of Seville's *Synonyma* and *Sententiae*, and Cross has clearly shown that these were not only known to

---

[1] *The Seafarer* (London, 1960), pp. 25-6; cf. also p. 12.

[2] H. M. Rochais, ' Contributions à l'histoire des florilèges ascétiques du haut moyen-âge ', *Revue bénédictine*, lxiii (1953), 246-91.

but used by Anglo-Saxon poets and homilists.[1]   The seventh-century *Liber Scintillarum* by Defensor was also popular and one copy has an interlinear Old English gloss.[2]   But of particular interest to us is the *speculum principis* or handbook of moral advice for a secular ruler, drawn up by the celebrated Anglo-Saxon scholar Alcuin at the court of Charlemagne.   It has been shown that he drew not only on Isidore but on the widely-disseminated seventh-century Irish tract *De Duodecim Abusivis Saeculi*, a number of pseudo-Augustinian homilies, Pomerius, Gregory, and Cassian.[3]

Irish Latin influence in Western Europe as a result of the missionary activities of Irish monks has long been recognised and recent research has shown a considerable body of biblical exegesis to be the work of Irish writers.[4]   The Irish appear to have had a particular fondness for the *speculum principis* from pagan times.   There are at least four collections of instructions to rulers, with only slight Christian influences, which go back at least to the eighth and ninth centuries, but are probably much older.   One of the most celebrated of these, the *Tecosca Cormaic* or *The Instructions of King Cormac MacAirt*, contains a passage strikingly similar in style and content to lines 66-8 of *The Wanderer*.   A Christian *speculum principis* occurs in the Irish MS., the *Leabhar Breac*, in a Latin version and also a somewhat expanded Irish one,[6] and bears the title *Sermo ad Reges*; it is an expansion of the ninth *abusivum* which treats of the Unjust King in the popular seventh-century Irish *florilegium, De Duodecim Abusivis Saeculi*.   One of the

[1] ' "Ubi Sunt " Passages in Old English—Sources and Relationships ', pp. 25-41.

[2] Edited by E. W. Rhodes for the Early English Text Society, Original Series 93 (London, 1889).

[3] Cf. L. Wallach, ' Alcuin on Virtues and Vices ', *Harvard Theological Review*, xlviii (1955), 175-95.

[4] B. Bischoff, ' Wendepunkte in der Geschichte der lateinischen Exegese im Frühmittelalter ', *Sacris Erudiri*, vi (1954), 189-281.

[5] K. Meyer, *The Instructions of King Cormac MacAirt*, Royal Irish Academy, Todd Lecture Series, volume xv (Dublin, 1909), p. 45.

[6] R. Atkinson, *The Passions and the Homilies from Leabhar Breac*, Royal Irish Academy, Todd Lecture Series, vol. ii (Dublin, 1887), pp. 151-62 (Irish text), 401-13 (translation of Irish text), 414-18 (Latin text).

interpolations is of special interest as it has a version of Isidore's *ubi sunt* motif which is closer to that contained in *The Seafarer* 80-4 and in Vercelli homily X than any yet suggested, namely the phrase *qui fuerunt ante te* corresponding to *swylce iū wǣron* (*Seafarer* 83) and *þā þe giō wǣron* (Vercelli X), and ' that were before thee of yore ' (translation of the Irish version). The Irish version is notable also for having discarded, like *The Seafarer*, the rhetorical questions of the motif; it has, moreover, points in common with passages in *The Wanderer*:

> Let him not exhibit vainglory nor pride, but let him subdue and humble himself, owing to the inconstancy and transitoriness of earthly rule: brief the time till worldly happiness decays; the riches and prosperity of this life are troublous and sorrow-fraught. Slight and perishable is earthly power; transitory and fragile, unstable and temporary, are lordship and power in this world. ' Take note, O king ', saith the sage, ' how swiftly have gone to nothingness the kings and emperors, the leaders and princes, that were before thee of yore in the highest estate and pre-eminence in this life. See for thyself the death and unhappy sequel of the rich and well-born: they found glory and exalted position in the world, but they all vanished like shadow or mist; they faded away like the vain images that are shown to men in dreams; and to a little consideration there is abundant example of decay, in the fact that no traces remain this day of their glory nor of their honour.' [1]

Much of the second part of *The Wanderer* is a concrete illustration of this theme, and lines 50-5 may be regarded as an expansion of ' they faded away as the vain images that are shown to men in dreams '. It cannot, of course, be demonstrated that the *Wanderer* poet knew or used this particular text; what is of interest is that as we move away from the *ubi sunt* formula of Isidore through the Latin-Irish version to the vernacular Irish we come closer to the atmosphere and phraseology of the Old English poems.

The Irish *De Duodecim Abusivis Saeculi* itself is of interest, for it contains in the second *abusivum* on the old man without

[1] R. Atkinson, *op. cit.* p. 410.

religion a close parallel with *The Seafarer* 91-6, as well as other similarities of subject matter.[1] The text was not only known to Alcuin but to a contemporary Englishman, Cathwulf, who alludes to it in a letter to Charlemagne.[2] Its wide popularity is probably due to the fact that it was commonly attributed to Cyprian and occasionally to Augustine.[3] The careful balancing of clauses and the lists of contrasting elements are stylistic features of this homily and characteristic of Irish writers. The extent to which the early Anglo-Saxon church came under the influence of Irish Christianity has been amply demonstrated.[4] It is of considerable interest that among the early Christian Latin poets whose preoccupations with the themes of death, decay and the brevity of human happiness are discussed by Mrs. Gordon,[5] the one who is most akin to the Old English poets of *The Wanderer* and *The Seafarer* is the Irish missionary monk, Columbanus, whose travels took him to Gaul, Austria and Italy; the opening lines of his precepts in the poem *De Vanitate et Miseria Vitae Mortalis* [6]

> Mundus iste transit, et
> Quotidie decrescit,
> Nemo vivens manebit,
> Nullus vivus remansit.

are very similar to lines 61-3 of *The Wanderer*.

[1] Cf. R. F. Leslie, *An Edition of the Old English Elegiac Poems ' The Wanderer ' and ' The Seafarer '*, *with a Study of Old English Elegiac Poetry*. Unpublished Ph.D. dissertation. Manchester, 1955.

[2] *Monumenta Germaniae Historica*, Epistolae iv, pp. 502-5. Allusion to it in Ælfric and in eleventh- and twelfth-century Old English homilies is documented by Mrs. J. Turville-Petre, *Arkiv för Nordisk Filologi*, lxxv (1960), 176.

[3] M. L. W. Laistner, *Thought and Letters in Western Europe*, 2nd edition, (London, 1957), pp. 145-6.

[4] See Laistner, *op. cit.* pp. 136 ff., Nora K. Chadwick, ' The Celtic Background of Early Anglo-Saxon England ', *Celt and Saxon: Studies in the Early British Border* (Cambridge, 1963), pp. 323-52, and G. W. Dunleavy, *Colum's Other Island, The Irish at Lindisfarne* (Madison, Wisconsin, 1960).

[5] *The Seafarer*, pp. 14, 22-3.

[6] *Patrologia Latina* LXXX, column 293.

The outlook of *The Wanderer* and *The Seafarer* is seen to be very similar to that of Latin Christian poems and homilies of the sixth to the ninth centuries, particularly those of Irish provenance; many of their motifs are the same—yet verbal parallels are few, and not extended. It is clear that the Anglo-Saxon poets have displayed a high degree of artistic competence in assimilating material from this common background to their own poetic medium and their own outlook. In perhaps the most stereotyped of the motifs, the *ubi sunt*, it is not the use of the motif which is surprising, but the extent of its adaptation to the heroic background most natural to Old English poetic diction.

The broad theme of both these poems is the transitoriness of this world and all that is in it. The principal divergences of opinion arise from the different emphases placed on the purposes for which this theme is used. Cross sees the genre of *The Wanderer* as *consolatio* and his thesis has the merit of being demonstrable of passages in both halves of the poem.[1] Smithers' demonstration of the ' essentially eschatological ' nature of the latter part of the poem, adds another dimension to it but leaves out of account the apparently much more personal first part, except in so far as it conforms to the symbolism of man as an exile from Paradise, discussed below.[2] Stanley sees the poem as directly related to informal penitential poetry,[3] and Lumiansky and Erzgräber as exemplifying the Boethian philosophy of the ' consolation ' of the true felicity of the supreme good or God.[4] Aspects of all these genres are undoubtedly represented in *The Wanderer*, and in no simple manner, for at least one of the motifs, the central *ubi sunt* passage, set off by being attributed to ' a wise man ' for emphasis,[5] is to be found associated with them all.

We should beware of placing too much emphasis on the

[1] ' On the Genre of *The Wanderer* ', *Neophilologus*, xlv (1961), 63-72.

[2] G. V. Smithers, ' The Meaning of *The Seafarer* and *The Wanderer*', *Medium Aevum*, xxvi (1957), 137-53 and xxviii (1959), 1-22.

[3] E. G. Stanley, *Anglia*, lxxiii (1955), 462-6.

[4] *Neophilologus*, xxxiv (1950), 109-11, and Erzgräber, *loc. cit.* pp. 57-85.

[5] Cf. the *ubi sunt* passage in the Irish version of the *Sermo ad Reges*, above, p. 28.

didactic aspects of the poem, for we would not only exclude some of its many dimensions, but would also fail to take account of the links with a non-Christian past which enrich the texture of the poem. There is a danger that enthusiasm for the discovery of the richness of the Christian background may obscure the fact that in Anglo-Saxon England ' a violent conversion to the new religion was unnecessary when the old provided so many parallelisms that the tribal culture could absorb the conquering God without disrupting many of its basic preconceptions '.[1]

The relationship between the second part of the poem and the first fifty-eight lines with their apparent realism and intensity of personal experience has been re-examined by the ' pan-allegorical school ' of critics as they have been called.[2] Basing themselves upon the multi-level biblical exegesis of Augustine and others, deriving from Origen, they have maintained that in Christian poems ' personal experience ' is postulated for the purpose of allegorical interpretation. Although these critics have given us valuable new insight into the effects of the exegetical traditions of the Church Fathers upon medieval writers, they appear to have failed to make an adequate distinction between full-blown *allegory*, in which an object or person exists only for the sake of the thing it signifies, and *typology*, in which a person, event or utterance has a significance other than the literal one, but nevertheless retains all its original meaning and value.[3]

The tendency to see *The Wanderer* and *The Seafarer* only in terms of allegory has led to a denial of any realism in the earlier voyage sections of both. There is also the implication that admiration of the apparently realistic passages is somewhat old-fashioned: ' The appeal of these poems does indeed seem to be enduring, but what appeals in them differs in every age. If one may speculate on how the poems were first received, one might guess that the Anglo-Saxons loved their wisdom to which we give the appellation " commonplaces ";

[1] W. A. Chaney, ' Paganism to Christianity in Anglo-Saxon England ', *Harvard Theological Review*, liii (1960), 209.

[2] By Charles Donahue in *Critical Approaches to Medieval Literature*, edited by Dorothy Bethurum, New York, 1960, p. 61.

[3] Cf. Donahue, *loc. cit.* pp. 64-6 and 160.

our immediate predecessors were moved by the imaginative
and lyrical terms of personal experience in part of these poems;
and we, accepting them wholly, admire in them the obliqueness
of approach in which and by which they are unities.' [1]   Modern
scholarship has undoubtedly added a dimension to our understanding of them, but only a dogmatic allegorical interpretation need prevent us from enjoying both the obliqueness
of the approach and acknowledging a starting-point in
the personal experience of the poet, however diversified and
expanded thereafter by literary conventions and stereotypes.
If we take account of typology we may have both lyricism and
symbolism, not simply through a romantic hankering after
realism, but through a recognition of the failure of a thorough-
going allegorical interpretation to account for all aspects of
the poem. There is, moreover, a real danger of making the
text fit the allegory.[2] D. W. Robertson, Jr., one of the
pioneers in the application of patristic exegesis to Old and
Middle English texts, makes a number of assumptions about
The Wanderer based upon textual interpretations which are not
unequivocal.[3] He claims that in the opening lines the pilgrim or
exile in the world faces difficulties as he prays to God for mercy
and confronts the trials of Fortune. But a good case can be
made for the *ānhaga* knowing nothing of God, but yet receiving
the uncovenanted mercy of God. While he does not deny the
Germanic ring of the description of the *eardstapa* in lines 6-7,
he maintains that because the wayfaring Christian is also a
warfaring Christian, the poet is describing the *eardstapa's*
battle against Satan. Although such an interpretation must
remain a possibility, we may not accept it without reservations
in view of the highly stereotyped nature of the description of
the *eardstapa*, entrenched in Old English poetic diction and
with strong heroic overtones. Its use for allegorical purposes
is not precluded on that account, but it would require from the

[1] E. G. Stanley, review of *The Seafarer* by Ida L. Gordon, *Medium
Aevum*, xxxi (1962), 55.

[2] R. E. Kaske, ' Chaucer and Medieval Allegory ', a Review Article
on D. W. Robertson, Jr., *A Preface to Chaucer; Studies in Medieval
Perspectives*, *ELH*, xxx (1963), 181.

[3] D. W. Robertson, Jr., ' Historical Criticism ', *English Institute
Essays 1950*, edited by Alan S. Downer (New York, 1951), pp. 18-19.

context support which it does not appear to have. Robertson goes on to describe the *wērig mōd* and *hrēo hyge* of lines 15 and 16 as the twin evils of despair and overconfidence of St. Augustine's sermons; but it is at least arguable that *wērigmōd* is a compound adjective here and that *hrēo* means ' sad ' troubles rather than ' fierce '. Discussing the *eardstapa's* burial of his lord (22-3), he states that the meaning of this would have been clear to a medieval audience as baptism, for baptism is a participation in the burial of Christ (Romans 6.3-6), and the exile of the Christian in the world begins with baptism. The wanderings of the *eardstapa* in search of a lord and his memories of the past (lines 25 ff.) are then to be interpreted as his thoughts of his own fleeting union with Christ at baptism and his dreams of embracing his Lord again when he finds Him a King in heaven as He was once a King on earth. Only the search for his Lord appears to have positive support from the poem; the reference to the search for one who would comfort the wanderer (28) finds reinforcement for its symbolism in the emphasis on the *frōfre* of the Heavenly Father in the last line of the poem, and the emphasis on the inconsolability of the lonely man in face of the unsubstantial nature of his attempts to evoke the past (34-58) finds an echo in the emphasis in the last line of the poem on the stability of God and heaven. We can, therefore, establish *typologies*, numbers of separate allusions deriving support from echoes in the poem and from words like *dryhten* whose ambiguity is manifest in Old English poetic diction; but this is a far cry from ' the continuous level of meaning beyond the literal ' [1] which allegory presupposes. One might fully endorse Robertson's conclusion: ' Nothing could be more mistaken than the usual notion that Old English literature exists in a kind of peculiar Germanic isolation from the rest of medieval literature. On the contrary it is in the Old English poetry that the general themes and the poetic techniques of medieval literature are first established in a vernacular.' [2] Nevertheless, it would be equally mistaken to assert that poems like *The Wanderer* and *The Seafarer* exist in a kind of peculiar patristic isolation from other Old English and Germanic poetry. We are

[1] Cf. R. E. Kaske, *loc. cit.* p. 192.   [2] *Op. cit.* p. 23.

not called upon to make an all-or-nothing choice between allegory and realism, and we need to bear in mind that it is possible to be quite as subjective about the former as about the latter.

In addition to classical and Latin Christian writings as possible influences upon the poet, Welsh or Irish secular poetry has also to be considered. Recent studies have added to the weight of evidence in favour of cultural intercourse between the Anglo-Saxons and the British Celts.[1] It seems likely that the children of mixed marriages would have some acquaintance with the rich literary heritage of their Celtic mothers. We know also of the traffic of Anglo-Saxon scholars to Ireland; it is not clear, however, whether their studies were confined to Latin or whether, in some cases, they embraced the vernacular as well. What can be said is that the group of elegiac lyrics in Old English in which *The Wanderer* is generally included, show a fondness for certain motifs which are of frequent occurrence in Celtic poetry.

The motif of the ruined hall or court (*The Wanderer* 75-87, 97-105) is one which appears in fifth- and sixth-century Gaul in the Latin writings of the Romanised Celts who were feeling the full impact of the Germanic invasions. The poignant expression which it took in their literature may well have been due to the Celtic imagination.[2] The motif appears in its most highly wrought form in the poetry of Venantius Fortunatus, which has been suggested as a possible literary source for its treatment in *The Wanderer*.[3] Likewise in Celtic Britain the reverses of the native inhabitants at the hands of the encroaching Anglo-Saxons find expression in elegies in which, as Mrs. Gordon states, ' the ruin theme is always a part of the theme of exile '.[4] But the concept of ruined cities was, of course, a commonplace of classical and later Christian Latin literature,[5] which could therefore be claimed as the poet's source. Moreover, the

[1] Cf. particularly Nora K. Chadwick, ' The Celtic Background of Early Anglo-Saxon England ', *Celt and Saxon: Studies in the Early British Border* (Cambridge, 1963), pp. 323-52.

[2] Nora K. Chadwick, *Poetry and Letters in Early Christian Gaul* (London, 1955), pp. 122-6.

[3] A. Brandl, ' Venantius Fortunatus und die ags. Elegien *Wanderer* und *Ruine* ', *Archiv*, cxxxix (1919), 84.   [4] *The Seafarer*, p. 20.

[5] J. E. Cross, ' On the Genre of *The Wanderer* ', pp. 68-72.

motif of the homeless wanderer and that of the ruined hall are not so integrated with each other in *The Wanderer* as they are in Welsh elegy because the Old English poet is, in the homiletic tradition, universalising his theme. Nevertheless, in his elaboration of the ruin motif he is more akin to the Celtic poets than to the classical and later Christian homilists.

Another feature which Celtic poetry and the Old English lyrics have in common is a close relationship between feelings and setting, as displayed in the first fifty-eight lines of *The Wanderer*, as well as in *The Husband's Message*, *The Wife's Lament* and *The Seafarer*. One aspect of this relationship is the occasional vignette of nature, such as the wanderer's description of seabirds bathing and preening in the wintry sea (lines 46-8). Spontaneous and acute observation of the things of nature was a special gift of Celtic poets.[1] Their poetry is richer in this respect than that of the Anglo-Saxons, who are often much more formal. The kinship of Celtic and Anglo-Saxon poets in natural observation is not, however, to be dismissed by pointing out that the effective presentation of the seabirds in *The Seafarer*, for example, ' appears in a series of rhetorical antitheses '.[2] These poets are fond of the counterpoint achieved by putting emotionally charged concepts within formal frameworks.[3] Occasionally a compelling case for the interaction of Celtic and Old English poetry can be made out, as with the cuckoo motif in *The Husband's Message*[4]; moreover, the elaboration in both of the ruin motif, the rapport between man and nature, together with a predilection for interweaving gnomic utterances with personal reflections,[5] make

[1] Cf. Mrs. Gordon, *The Seafarer*, p. 20 and K. Jackson, *Early Celtic Nature Poetry* (Cardiff, 1935), pp. 79-175.

[2] J. E. Cross, Review of *The Seafarer* by Mrs. Gordon in *JEGP*, lx (1961), 547.   [3] See Notes to lines 92-6, 108-9.

[4] R. F. Leslie, *Three Old English Elegies* (Manchester, 1961), p. 61.

[5] K. Jackson, *op. cit.* pp. 127-48. In an article published after this edition went to press, ' The Elegiac Genre in Old English and Early Welsh Poetry,' *Zeitschrift für Celtische Philologie*, xxix (1964), 209-24, Herbert Pilch points to the *Claf Abercuawg*, from the Red Book of Hergest, as the single early Welsh poem which comes closest to the elegiac genre of Old English. He indicates a number of motifs which it has in common with *The Wanderer* (*loc. cit.* pp. 213-15).

the possibility of some interaction between them more likely than not. The particularly Celtic contribution to Old English poetry appears to have been of pattern rather than of content. A liking for a particular blend of ingredients was probably transmitted orally, independently of specific models, unlike the Latin Christian influence, which is much more formal and demonstrably literary.

The emphasis on voyaging as an elegiac motif in both *The Wanderer* and *The Seafarer* is not, however, to be explained as of Celtic origin.[1] There are two arguments in favour of a ' native ' origin for this feature. One is the striking attachment of Anglo-Saxon poets to descriptions of voyages against a background of stormy seascapes; these are often enlarged upon for their own sakes, as in *Andreas* 369-81, 438-48, as if the mere mention of a voyage were enough to set the poet off on this tack. A second argument is the density of stereotyped formulaic phrases in such passages. The techniques devised by Parry and Lord in the study of orally transmitted poetry in Eastern Europe, as applied by Magoun and others, have provided us with the means of discerning those elements in an Anglo-Saxon poem which are traditional in form and subject matter.[2] Techniques of alliterative poetry and forms of poetic diction forged in pre-literate days were the instruments at the command of the Anglo-Saxon poets when the coming of literacy gave some of their work a permanent form, regardless of whether they in fact continued to compose orally or with pen in hand. The themes of exile, battle, the sea and the lord-retainer relationship have been particularly fertile for the production of stereotypes.

Although it is difficult to speak with precision of sources, except probably in the case of the *ubi sunt* and *sum . . . sum* formulas, *The Wanderer* appears to contain a blend of traditional Germanic themes and images and themes derived from

[1] Cf. Mrs. Gordon, *The Seafarer*, p. 21.

[2] F. P. Magoun, Jr., ' Oral-Formulaic Character of Anglo-Saxon Narrative Poetry ', *Speculum*, xxviii (1953), 446-67, J. J. Campbell, ' Oral Poetry in *The Seafarer* ', *Speculum*, xxxv (1960), 87 ff., W. A. O'Neil, *Oral-Formulaic Structure in Old English Elegiac Poetry*. Dis., University of Wisconsin, 1960, and R. D. Stevick, ' The Oral-Formulaic Analyses of Old English Verse ', *Speculum*, xxxvii (1962), 382-9.

Boethius and the Christian Latin literature emanating from Irish writers, or writers influenced by the traditions, techniques and interests of Irish Christianity. Celtic vernacular influence on the poet is more difficult to define, involving as it does, the scope and emphasis which the poet has given to themes already to hand rather than the adoption of new ones. It remains an open question, moreover, how far some features of the Celtic impress, particularly the relationship between man and his natural setting and the fondness for cumulative or antithetical rhetorical devices, may have been derived either from Gaulish Latin writers or the Latin poetry and prose of Irish monks and missionaries.

POETIC ACHIEVEMENT

The Wanderer has deservedly been praised for its pictures of lowering storm, winter seas and desolate landscape. Nevertheless, the complexity and subtlety of the poet's achievement have been underestimated because the right features have been praised for the wrong reasons. One critic, for example, writes approvingly that ' one root of the modernity of atmosphere which characterises the poem is the faithful depiction of nature. This realism, though selective in detail, derives not from literary convention but from first-hand and observant contact with the external world '.[1] In an age which has ceased to apologise for the irrefutably medieval in pre-Renaissance literature and is attempting to understand it in terms of its own conventions and philosophy, to praise a medieval poem for its modernity of atmosphere is almost to damn it. The depiction of nature is certainly faithful, but the stereotyped nature of much of the imagery points rather to inherited literary conventions than to first-hand observation. To limit the poet's scope is not, however, to deny to him altogether the freshness of first-hand experience, which appears to have prompted the picture of the seabirds in line 47 and his acute awareness of the tricks the imagination plays on a solitary wanderer in a monotonous environment. His powerful resurrection of the past (lines

[1] C. W. Kennedy, *Earliest English Poetry* (New York, 1943), p. 106.

34-57) increases in intensity from memory through dream to hallucination of the visible presence of the wandering man's kinsmen; but the phantoms are mute and grief is renewed for the man who is doomed to constant lonely voyaging.

Even where many of the sea and storm images are conventional they are carefully selected to match the bleakness and desolation of the wanderer himself; they are also impressively marshalled to serve both as a backdrop to the destruction of man and as agents of the obliteration of his works. There is both symbolism and realism. The natural setting is used also as an effective counterpoint to the exile's dream of past joys in the company of his lord; a sudden contrast is provided in lines 45-50a when he reawakens to the bleak realities of the present, made all the more poignant by the portrayal of his actual companions in the seascape, the birds of line 47 which provide a focal point in the waste of waters. The author of *The Seafarer* achieves similar effects by the introduction of seabirds in lines 19-22, although in a notably different way; his exile figure hears the birds and the waves, whereas the exile in *The Wanderer* observes them. The emphasis throughout the poem is on the visual, as in the hallucination (50-5), the ruins (73-7, 97-8), and the words for darkness: *gesweorce* (59), *þis deorce līf* (89), *genāp under nihthelm* (96), *nīpeð nihtscūa* (104).

The poet makes use of many of the poetic themes of his age, other than those which spring from warfare. There are references to battle and the introduction of typical battle imagery in lines 7, 78-80, 90-1 and 99-100; but the references are brief, they are not developed as a theme and are introduced solely as the distant reason for a present state of affairs. The poet is much more interested in effects than in the actions which cause them, as the brevity of the wanderer's personal history confirms; in barely four lines (22-5) we have his biography, a minimal account to explain his status as an exile wanderer whose state of mind, expectations and disappointments are the central points of interest and exploration. The subordination of his personal history and the expression of the wanderer's misery by means of stereotyped imagery emphasise the typical elements of the exile's plight, and ease the transition to the sustained generalisation of lines 29b-57. A recognition of this approach makes largely irrelevant the discussion whether there is a ' real ' wanderer or only a symbolic figure, for the poet obtains the best of both worlds by giving his character individuality enough to gain our sympathy, but not enough for the idiosyncrasies of an individual history to interfere with the experiences of the exile wanderer type.

We may ask why the poet, once launched on generalised experience, should choose to reincarnate the wanderer in the first person, in lines 58-62, for such a brief appearance. The answer is to be found in the limitations imposed upon the typical exile wanderer, imprisoned by a frustration and despair which even the most intense flights of man's imagination are powerless to transcend (50-5). The wanderer differs at this point from the type because he can set *pās woruld* (58) in perspective with the eternal world. He cannot do so simply because he is wise and experienced, for he goes on to point out from lines 62b to 110 that although earthly wisdom can apprehend the universality of decay it can take us no further. When we enquire whence came his insight, we see the significance of the opening lines of the poem; he is an *ānhaga* who not only has long had to wander on the rime-cold sea but who has experienced God's mercy. The individual is brought forward again in order to dissociate him, in this one vital respect, from both the typical exile wanderer and the man wise in the ways of this world alone.

Anglo-Saxon poetry, with its kennings, compounds and variants tends to be somewhat formal, but this inherent formality is of a kind rather different from that of the rhetorical devices of which the poet makes occasional effective use. The parallelism of the *nāles* phrases in lines 32-3 comes at the climax of the introduction of the exile wanderer and his situation, before his state of mind is discussed. A parallelism of a different order is that between *Sorg bið genīwad* (50b) and *Cearo bið genīwad* (55b), the first anticipating the bitterness of disappointment when the mirage is identified, the second indicating the return of the exile to a state of grief and hardship, doubly hard to bear after the false hopes which have been raised. The complex *ne tō* series (66-9) occurs at a turning point in the poem; here the hallmarks of the wise man are enumerated, with the emphasis on moderation and prudence. Here

4

the gnomic elements, native and perhaps influenced by Celtic literature also, are integrated with Christian precepts, many deriving ultimately from the Book of Proverbs, which would be within the ready comprehension of the ' noble pagan ' of the type presented so vividly by the *Beowulf* poet in Hroðgar.[1] The prominence of moderation as a concomitant of wisdom is subscribed to by St. Martin of Braga who, in his *Formula Honestae Vitae*,[2] has not only sections on prudence, magnanimity, continence and justice, but sections *de mensura et moderatione* on each of these virtues.

The importance of the *ubi sunt* passage (92-6) as an embodiment of traditional heroic concepts within a Christian formula has been indicated above. As a rhetorical device it fulfils several functions; it provides an emotional peak for the survey of this world by the wanderer's postulated wise man; its contents touch off a whole range of reactions to the central aspects of the lord-retainer relationship and the heroic way of life; and, for the reader familiar with Christian homiletic literature, it clearly signposts the road the poet is about to take, towards an injunction to turn to God, since all earthly joys are transitory. The final rhetorical passage, with the repeated *hēr bið . . . lǣne* phrases (108-9), also comes at the culmination of a section, that dealing with the desolation of the whole world; like the *ubi sunt* passage it is designed to have both traditional and Christian overtones.

The last six lines of the poem have a special emphasis in that they are verses of the extended hypermetric type which occur, sometimes singly, sometimes in groups, in a number of Old English poems. They are most frequent in poems in which the preceptual content is high, particularly in *Maxims I* and *II* and *Solomon and Saturn*. This kind of verse appears to have been considered especially fitting for gnomic and other didactic poetry, which seems to belong, in some respects, to a

[1] Cf. Morton W. Bloomfield, ' Patristics and Old English Literature: Notes on Some Poems ', *Studies in Old English Literature in Honor of Arthur G. Brodeur* (University of Oregon, 1963), p. 39: ' The tendency to assimilate the best part of paganism to the Old Testament is one way converted pagans could accept the New Law and still maintain pride of ancestry.'

[2] *Patrologia Latina*, LXXII, cols. 21-8.

different tradition from the rest, and especially in the concluding lines of a poem as here and in *Judith*.[1]

An outstanding feature of the diction of *The Wanderer* is the number of unique or unusual words, more than forty in 115 lines of poetry. Many do not appear remarkable because they are compounds constructed from familiar elements, combined according to familiar patterns, such as *brimfuglas* 47, *feohgífre* 68, *hæglfare* 105, *selesecgas* 34 and *wintercearig* 24. Some are probably of the poet's own creation; others would no doubt be recognised as regular elements of the poetic vocabulary if more Old English poetry had survived.[2] Several of the rare words are adjectives denoting sadness: *dréorighléor* 83, *módcearig* 2, *seledréorig* 25, *wintercearig* 24 and *earmcearig* 20 (elsewhere only in *The Seafarer* 14). The early part of the poem is particularly rich in adjectives denoting personal distress; there are no fewer than nine in lines 15-33. The poet's skill in choosing words appropriately can be demonstrated in his words for ' lord ' in lines 22-44; twice *goldwine* is used when the wanderer is referring to his original lord as friend and patron; *sinces bryttan* (25) has not the affectionate ties denoted by *wine-* compounds, and is a phrase denoting his expectations of a new lord as a source of patronage; *winedryhtnes* (37) is his old lord again in the role of mentor; and *mondryhten* (41) is his liege lord to whom he paid homage.

Its imagery bears out the description of *The Wanderer* as an elegiac poem. The poet makes full use of all the features of the exile formula in Old English poetry, when he introduces the exile wanderer in lines 1-5, and more abundantly in lines 20-33, the heart of the personal elegy, in which the major features of the formula are all represented [3]; namely the exile's sadness or wretchedness, his lonely and friendless state, an account of the events that led to his exile, often with a brief but vivid description of his present environment, and his deprivation of home and possessions. The whole personal

[1] B. J. Timmer, ' Expanded Lines in Old English Poetry ', *Neophilologus*, xxxv (1952), 226-30, and A. J. Bliss, *The Metre of Beowulf* (Oxford, 1958), pp. 96-7.

[2] Cf. E. G. Stanley, Anglia lxxiii (1955), pp. 444-5.

[3] Cf. S. B. Greenfield, ' The Formulaic Expression of the Theme of " Exile " in Anglo-Saxon Poetry ', *Speculum*, xxx (1955), 200-6.

elegy (8-36) is similar in tone to *The Wife's Lament*, with which
its fluent style and economical diction are comparable. It
also has considerable similarity in outlook and diction to the
passage towards the close of *Guthlac*, lines 1325-65, where the
disciple travels by sea, grieving for his dead lord, and addresses
to the latter's sister a speech which, like *The Wanderer* passage,
is full of images of deprivation and of the necessity to take the
exile's path. The style is turgid in places but is at its most
lucid and direct in that section which corresponds most closely
to the personal elegy in our poem.

The very abundance of stereotyped imagery in Old English
makes an appropriate choice, or adaptation, a matter of considerable art. Although the needs of alliteration played their
part in the poet's choice of words, he was nevertheless free to
choose within a wide range. Since key concepts were realised
by a variety of synonyms, a mechanically dictated choice need
rarely have been forced upon a good poet, whose choice of one
word rather than another can therefore be claimed to have
significance, not only in passages of considerable originality
but in those filled with inherited images. A sensitive and
competent poet such as the author of *The Wanderer* can obtain
by judicious choice of images and variant expressions, and of
the syntactical forms in which to incorporate them, a wide
range of stylistic effects to match the contents of particular
passages. In addition, there are opportunities for varying
emphasis afforded by the alliterative verse form itself. The
accumulation of verbal phrases with a single object in lines
51-2 emphasises the impress being made upon the imagination
of the passive but receptive exile. In lines 76-7 the parallel
participial phrases in the first half-lines, both qualifying *weallas*,
give a pattern of emphasis of quite a different kind.[1]

The impersonal elegy in *The Wanderer* has, like the personal
elegy, its distinctive structure and its Old English analogues.
Most of *The Ruin* and the speech of the last survivor in *Beowulf*
2247-66, are of this type. The subject is a vanished race or
tribe, the main description is of possessions or buildings left

[1] See also the stylistic study of lines 19-29 by S. B. Greenfield,
' Syntactic Analysis and Old English Poetry ', *Neuphilologische Mitteil-
ungen*, lxiv (1963), 373-8 and ' Verse Syntax and its Relationship to
Formula ', W. A. O'Neil, *op. cit.* pp. 82-136.

behind; there is generally a description of the agent of death, usually battle or pestilence, and a description of the martial glory and prowess of the vanished race. The principal motifs occur in lines 73-87 of *The Wanderer*. But already in line 74, by projecting his picture of desolation into the future, and by making God the agent of destruction at the end of the passage, the poet enlarges a theme whose emotional impact he has fully exploited, to give us a hint of the Last Judgment. The form of the *ubi sunt* passage confirms this transfer on to a homiletic plane while its contents provide continuity with what has gone before. As he proceeds to universalise the theme of the vanished race, the impressiveness of the decay of all creation is matched by the grim splendour of his last passage of natural description.

It can be seen from the foregoing analyses that the structure and imagery of *The Wanderer* are extremely complex. The poet is not writing exclusively on mutability and misery, although these are important elements; self-discipline, prudence and moderation are pervasive aspects of wisdom which give the poem something of the quality of a *speculum principis*. Basically this is a Christian poem, but it is not directed exclusively, or even primarily towards Christians. If it were, the criticism that too much attention is devoted to the problem of the beginnings and ends of speeches in the poem would be justified. The wanderer and the wise man are indeed embodiments of aspects of the poet's teaching, and much of what he wishes to convey is made part of their speeches; yet their function is not simply to provide artistic variation. Much of the confusion about the extent of the speeches has arisen from failure to recognise that they are not in series, but enclosed one within another; the most comprehensive view, the Christian one, is outside, and the less comprehensive, the ' heroic ' one, inside. The themes and motifs within the poem, as we have seen, reflect such a structure; this is obscured if we fail to take the opening and closing lines as belonging to the ' wanderer '. The poet speaks in unison with him; but he must have a wanderer, in order to avoid the charge of moralising without contact with reality. The wanderer is a moralist with the authority of experience, experience both of the pleasures of men and the hardships and sorrows of men, who has come to know God's mercy in the midst of exile. The wise man is in turn a projection of the wanderer's whose role is limited to the expression of a ' heroic ' point of view; he is the *wita* (65), the *glēaw hæle* (73), the *Sē . . . frōd in ferðe* (88-90). It is admittedly difficult for us clearly to distinguish the two because of the extent to which the Christian and ' heroic ' viewpoints overlap. Indeed much of the subtlety of the poem resides in the significance of their failure to coincide exactly. By a gradual shift of emphasis from the known to the unknown, a Christian poet, using the wanderer figure as a stalking-horse and the wise man as a decoy, is attempting to lead men of wisdom and fortitude into making an active search for God in that one aspect of His being in which He is demonstrably supreme, His fixed and unalterable nature, in contrast to the mutability of the world and its inhabitants so powerfully demonstrated throughout the greater part of the poem.

DIALECT AND DATE

The Exeter Book has generally been assigned to the last quarter of the tenth century and is believed to be a reproduction of an anthology put together earlier in the century. Scribes freely and often mechanically substituted forms to which they were accustomed for those in the copy before them; that the *Exeter Book* scribe was no exception can be clearly seen from the errors which he has made.[1] For the most part the language of *The Wanderer* is typical of that of *The Exeter Book* as a whole and the forms are predominantly those of the late West-Saxon dialect contemporary with the scribe. Here and there occur forms generally presumed to be foreign to this dialect; nevertheless, although most of these ' can be classified as phonologically or morphologically proper to one dialect or another, it is seldom possible to declare with confidence that a given poem was originally in a particular dialect, or even that it was non-West-Saxon '.[2] Uncertainty about the dialectal distribution of forms has been deepened by the doubts which

[1] K. Sisam, *Studies in the History of Old English Literature* (Oxford, 1953), pp. 98, 106.

[2] Alistair Campbell, *Old English Grammar* (Oxford, 1959), p. 10.

have been cast on the traditional assignation of certain key prose texts to particular dialects.[1]

There is a further difficulty in using forms as evidence of the date or dialect of composition of a poem; a poet might prefer to take his models from a common stock rather than from the relatively unknown work of his own district. ' In this way poems could be produced that do not belong to any local dialect, but to a general Old English poetic dialect, artificial, archaic, and perhaps mixed in its vocabulary, conservative in inflexions that affect the verse-structure, and indifferent to non-structural irregularities, which were perhaps tolerated as part of the colouring of the language of verse.'[2] The study of oral-formulaic elements in Old English poetry, which has flowered in the decade since Sisam's statement, has lent considerable support to his theory of a common stock.[3]

Nevertheless, an indication of the principal dialectal characteristics of the poem and a tentative assignation of those forms which appear to differ in date or dialect from the majority are not without interest even if, in the present state of Old English studies, they are of doubtful value as evidence of the date or dialect of the author of the poem.

Features of dialect interest include the following:

1. Characteristic early West Saxon *ie* appears only in the initial combination *gie*, in *cwidegiedda* 55, *giefstōlas* 44, *gielpes* 69, *ongietan* 73. This feature is shared with most of *The Exeter Book* [Sisam, p. 100].

2. Late West Saxon *y* from earlier *ie* occurs in *hyra* 18, *mappumgyfa* 92, *scyppend* 85; *y* for *i* earlier *e*, occurs in *gehwylce* 8, *ryccne* 112 [Sievers-Brunner, § 22, Anm. 2].

3. Characteristic of late West Saxon is the genitive singular of an *a* stem noun in *-as* in *giefstōlas* 44. As a result of the

---

[1] R. M. Wilson has shown that a Mercian provenance for the Vespasian Psalter glosses is by no means certain; *v. The Anglo-Saxons, Studies in some Aspects of their History and Culture,* presented to Bruce Dickins, London, 1959, pp. 280-310. In ' The Old English Bede ', *Proceedings of the British Academy* 1962, pp. 57-9, Dorothy Whitelock states the case for a Mercian origin for this ' Alfredian ' text.

[2] K. Sisam, *op. cit.* p. 138.

[3] For an analysis of the formulaic elements in the elegies see Wayne A. O'Neil, *op. cit.* pp. 1-75.

gradual weakening of vowels in final lightly stressed syllables, there was considerable scribal variation [Campbell § 379].

4. West Saxon *ǣ*, from West Germanic *ā*, occurs eighteen times in the poem; in the only example of non-West-Saxon *ē*, in *wēgas* 46, the form may have been read as *wegas* and so have escaped alteration [Campbell §128].

5. In West Saxon *æ* was fractured to *ea* before *l* + consonant, but remained unfractured in Anglian and was later retracted to *a*. Of the fourteen relevant forms in the poem, twelve show fracture. Two which do not are *waldend* 78, and *ælda* 85 (where earlier *a* has undergone front mutation). These forms are, however, common in poetic texts and were probably part of the general literary stock [Sievers-Brunner, § 85; Campbell, § 143].

6. *ea/eo* confusion of *eo* and *ea* is found regularly in Northumbrian [Sievers-Brunner, § 35, Anm. 1; Campbell, § 278(b)], but occurs sporadically in West Saxon and the Vespasian Psalter Gloss [Campbell, § 281]; cf. *wearþan* 64, with the more usual *weorþan*.

7. Back mutation of *e* to *eo* before *d, t, þ* did not take place in West Saxon but was widespread in Anglian, as in *meoduhealle* 27, *sweotule* 11, and *stānhleoþu* 101. Unmutated are *metudes* 2, *ederas* 77 (earlier *edoras*) and *gesetu* 93 [Luick, § 228b; Sievers-Brunner, § 110, Anm. 1; Campbell, § 210].

8. In West Saxon *u* in a final lightly stressed syllable early became *o* before consonants other than *m* or *ng* when not preceded by *u* in the stem syllable, whereas it remained in early Northumbrian and extensively in Mercian; *u* is retained in *metudes* 2, *sweotule* 11, *weoruld* 107, but has become *o* or *e* in *hēafod* 43, *ederas* 77, *feterum* 21, *fugel* 81, *waþema* 24, 57 [Sievers-Brunner, § 44, Anm. 7; Campbell, § 373].

9. Syncope in the 2nd and 3rd person singular present indicative of strong verbs has generally been held to be characteristic of West Saxon, and lack of syncope to be characteristic of Anglian. But Sisam (*loc. cit.* pp. 123-5) has shown the unreliability of this tenet for poetry and states that all the evidence is consistent with the view that the uncontracted endings were general in Old English in early centuries, and were regarded as appropriate to verse, at least to the end of the tenth century,

by writers for whom the short forms were normal in prose. All such forms in the poem are uncontracted, except *gesihð* 46. [See also Sievers-Brunner, § 374; Campbell, § 733-734.]

10. Weak verbs of Class 2, which usually form their past participles with *-od* in West Saxon, have *-ad* in Anglian, as *geniwad* 50, 55 [Sievers-Brunner, § 413, Anm. 6; Campbell, § 757].

In common with most poems in *The Exeter Book*, and indeed most ' classical ' Old English poetry, the language of *The Wanderer* is for the most part late West Saxon, but it also contains early West Saxon forms, a number of ' poetic ' forms possibly Anglian in origin, and forms which appear to be Anglian and could be the result either of transmission at some time by an Anglian scribe or of original composition in an Anglian dialect.

No greater precision is possible about the date of composition of the poem. Many of the metrical and linguistic criteria formerly used to establish the approximate date of composition of an Old English poem have been shown to be inconclusive.[1]

A *terminus ad quem* for the composition of the poem is fixed by the date of *The Exeter Book* itself, some time during the second half of the tenth century.[2] Sisam, however, suggests that the anthology was put together during the first half of the century.[3] As with many Old English poems, a *terminus a quo* is not easy to establish; but there is general agreement that none of the poems such as *Beowulf*, *The Seafarer* and *The Wanderer*, in which traditional and Christian motifs are well integrated, are likely to have been composed prior to the eighth century. Moreover, there do not appear to be any metrical or linguistic features of *The Wanderer* which require the consideration of a date of composition earlier than the eighth century.

Comparisons with other texts may be of value but must be made with caution, since different kinds of poetry might well

---

[1] Dorothy Whitelock, ' Anglo-Saxon Poetry and the Historian ', *Transactions of the Royal Historical Society*, xxxi (1949), 75-94, and *The Audience of Beowulf* (Oxford, 1951).

[2] Cf. Sisam, *op. cit.* p. 99, and N. R. Ker, *Catalogue of Manuscripts containing Anglo-Saxon* (Oxford, 1957), p. 153.   [3] *Op. cit.* p. 108.

have been written in different styles during the same period. The signed poems of Cynewulf are useful for comparison because there is a wide measure of agreement that he wrote during the first half of the ninth century. To be valid, comparisons with *The Wanderer* should be restricted to passages such as those towards the end of *Juliana* and *Elene* which contain many of the ingredients of *The Wanderer*, namely personal elegy, references to nature, and reflections on the transitoriness of this world. Cynewulf's handling of traditional imagery appears to be much more stylised and perfunctory than that of the *Wanderer* poet and to indicate a later date of composition. This impression is strengthened when a comparison is made between *The Wanderer* and *The Ruin* or the elegy of the last survivor in *Beowulf*. Here the treatment of elegiac themes and the flexibility of the verse are much closer to those of *The Wanderer*. Although the dates of these poems are not certain there are grounds for believing them to have been written in the eighth century.[1]

The facility and sensitivity of the poet's use of closely related compounds, many of them rare or unknown elsewhere,[2] also suggest composition in a period when variation of traditional imagery was still a living art. In Cynewulf's poetry much of the older imagery has become static and ornamental.

Another possible indication of the date when *The Wanderer* was composed may be seen in the poet's affinities with the writings and attitudes of the Irish-Latin homilists, whose influence in Western Europe extended from the seventh century to the period of Alcuin, towards the end of the eighth.

[1] See Dorothy Whitelock, *The Audience of Beowulf* (Oxford, 1951), and R. F. Leslie, *Three Old English Elegies*, p. 36.

[2] See above, p. 41.

SELECT BIBLIOGRAPHY

MANUSCRIPT AND FACSIMILE

BRITISH MUSEUM Additional MS. 9067. A transcript of the Exeter Book made by Robert Chambers in 1831 and collated by Sir Frederic Madden in 1832.

CHAMBERS, R. W., FÖRSTER, M. and FLOWER, R. *The Exeter Book of Old English Poetry.* Collotype facsimile. London, 1933.

KER, N. R. *Catalogue of Manuscripts containing Anglo-Saxon.* Oxford, 1957.

SISAM, K. 'The Exeter Book', *Studies in the History of Old English Literature.* Oxford, 1953, pp. 97-108.

EDITIONS

ANDERSON, MARJORIE and WILLIAMS, BLANCHE C. *Old English Handbook.* Boston, 1935.

BOLTON, W. F. *An Old English Anthology.* London, 1963.

BRIGHT, J. W. *An Anglo-Saxon Reader.* Fourth edition. London, 1903.

CRAIGIE, W. A. *Specimens of Anglo-Saxon Poetry, III. Germanic Legend and Anglo-Saxon History and Life.* Edinburgh, 1931.

ETTMÜLLER, L. *Engla and Seaxna Scôpas and Bôceras.* Quedlinburg and Leipzig, 1850.

FLOM, G. T. *Introductory Old English Grammar and Reader.* Boston, 1930.

GOLLANCZ, I. *The Exeter Book,* part I. EETS Original Series 104. London, 1895.

GREIN, C. W. M. *Bibliothek der angelsächsischen Poesie,* vol. I. Göttingen, 1857.

IMELMANN, R. *Forschungen zur altenglischen Poesie.* Berlin, 1920.

KAISER, R. *Alt- und mittelenglische Anthologie.* Third edition. Berlin, 1958.

KERSHAW, NORA. *Anglo-Saxon and Norse Poems.* Cambridge, 1922.

KLIPSTEIN, L. F. *Analecta Anglo-Saxonica,* vol. II. New York and London, 1849.

KLUGE, F. *Angelsächsisches Lesebuch.* Third edition. Halle, 1902.

KRAPP, G. P. and DOBBIE, E. V. K. *The Exeter Book*. The Anglo-Saxon Poetic Records, III. New York, 1936.

KRAPP, G. P. and KENNEDY, A. G. *An Anglo-Saxon Reader*. New York, 1929.

LEHNERT, M. *Poetry and Prose of the Anglo-Saxons*. London, 1957.

MARCH, F. A. *Introduction to Anglo-Saxon*. New York, 1870.

MOSSÉ, F. *Manuel de l'Anglais du Moyen Âge des origines au XIVe siècle*, I: Vieil-Anglais. Second edition. Paris, 1950.

RICCI, H. *L'Elegia Pagana Anglosassone*. Florence, 1923.

RIEGER, M. *Alt- und angelsächsisches Lesebuch*. Giessen, 1861.

SCHÜCKING, L. L. *Kleines angelsächsisches Dichterbuch*. Second edition. Leipzig, 1933.

SEDGEFIELD, W. J. *An Anglo-Saxon Verse-Book*. Manchester, 1922.

SETZLER, E. B. *The Jefferson Anglo-Saxon Grammar and Reader*. New York, 1938.

SIEPER, E. *Die altenglische Elegie*. Strassburg, 1915.

SMITH, C. A. *An Old English Grammar and Exercise Book*. Boston, 1898.

SWEET, H. *An Anglo-Saxon Reader in Prose and Verse*. Eighth edition. Oxford, 1908.

SWEET, H. *An Anglo-Saxon Reader in Prose and Verse*. Fifteenth edition, revised throughout by Dorothy Whitelock. Oxford, 1967.

THORPE, B. *Codex Exoniensis*. Published for the Society of Antiquaries. London, 1842.

TURK, M. H. *An Anglo-Saxon Reader*. New York, 1927.

WÜLKER, R. P. *Kleinere angelsächsische Denkmäler*. Halle, 1879.

WÜLKER, R. P. *Bibliothek der angelsächsischen Poesie*, vol. I. Begründet von Christian W. M. Grein. Kassel, 1883.

WYATT, A. J. *An Anglo-Saxon Reader*. Cambridge, 1919.

TRANSLATIONS

ABBOTT, C. C. 'Three Old English Elegies', *Durham University Journal*, xxxvi (N.S. V) (1943-4), 76-9.

COOK, A. S. and TINKER, C. B. *Select Translations from Old English Poetry*. Boston, 1926.

FAUST, COSETTE and THOMPSON, S. *Old English Poems*. Chicago, 1918.

FULTON, E. 'On Translating Old English Poetry', *PMLA*, xiii (1898), 286-96.

GORDON, R. K. *Anglo-Saxon Poetry*. London, 1927.

HICKEY, EMILY H. *'The Wanderer*. From the English of Cynewulf', *The Academy*, xix (1881), 355.

KENNEDY, C. W. *Old English Elegies*. Princeton, 1936.

KENNEDY, C. W. *An Anthology of Old English Poetry*. London and New York, 1960.

RAFFEL, BURTON. '"The Wanderer". New Translation', *London Magazine* (July 1959), pp. 22-4.

RAFFEL, BURTON. *Poems from the Old English*. Nebraska University Press, 1961.

SIMS, W. R. 'The Wanderer', *MLN*, v (1890), 402-4.

SPAETH, J. D. *Old English Poetry*. Princeton, 1922.

See also Thorpe, Gollancz, Sieper, Miss Kershaw, Lehnert and Mackie above, and Brooke (both works).

TEXTUAL STUDIES

ASHDOWN, MARGARET. '"The Wanderer" lines 41-3', *MLR*, xxii (1927), 313-14.

BOWEN, ROBERT O. 'The Wanderer, 98', *Explicator* xiii (1955), Item 26.

BREWER, D. S. 'Wanderer, lines 50-7', *MLN*, lxvii (1952), 398-9.

BRIGHT, J. W. 'The Wanderer 78-84', *MLN*, xiii (1898), 351-3.

CRAIGIE, W. A. 'Interpolations and omissions in Anglo-Saxon poetic texts', *Philologica*, ii (1923-4), 14-16.

DUBOIS, ARTHUR, E. 'Gifstol', *MLN*, lxix (1954), 546-9.

EKWALL, E. Review of Miss Kershaw's *Anglo-Saxon and Norse Poems* in *Anglia Beiblatt*, xxxv (1924), 133-5.

FISCHER, W. '*Wanderer* v. 25 und v. 6-7', *Anglia*, lix (1935), 299-302.

FRENCH, W. H. '"The Wanderer" 98: *wyrmlicum fāh*', *MLN*, lxvii (1952), 526-9.

GREENFIELD, STANLEY B. 'Syntactic Analysis and Old English Poetry', *Neuphilologische Mitteilungen*, lxiv (1963), 373-8.

GREIN, C. W. M. 'Zur Textkritik der angelsächsischen Dichter', *Germania*, x (1865), 421-2.

HEMPEL, H. *Untersuchungen zum Wanderer*. Halle, 1915.

HOLTHAUSEN, F. 'Zu alt- und mittelenglischen Dichtungen', *Anglia*, xiii (1891), 357.

HOLTHAUSEN, F. Review of Kock's *Jubilee Jaunts and Jottings* in *Anglia Beiblatt*, xxx (1919), 1-5.

HOLTHAUSEN, F. 'Studien zur altenglischen Dichtung: III. Zu Imelmann's Forschungen', *Anglia*, xlvi (1922), 56.

JACOBSEN, R. *Darstellung der syntaktischen Erscheinungen im angelsächsischen Gedichte vom Wanderer*. Dissertation. Rostock, 1901.

KLAEBER, F. 'Wanderer 44; Rätsel XII 3 f.', *Anglia Beiblatt*, xvii (1906), 300.

KLAEBER, F. 'Notes on Old English Poems 12', *JEGP*, xii (1913), 259-60.

KLAEBER, F. Review of Sedgefield's *An Anglo-Saxon Verse Book* in *JEGP*, xxiii (1924), 123-4.

KLAEBER, F. 'Jottings on Old English Poems', *Anglia*, liii (1929), 229.

KOCK, E. A. *Jubilee Jaunts and Jottings*. Lunds Universitet Arsskrift, N. F. Avd. 1. Bd. 14, Nr. 26. Lund, 1918, pp. 75-9.

LARSON, L. M. 'The Household of the Norwegian Kings', *American Historical Review*, xiii (1908), 439-79.

LEHMANN, W. 'Anmerkungen zum altenglischen Sprachschatz', *Archiv*, cxix (1907), 435.

LINDHEIM, B. von. 'OE "Drēam" and its subsequent Development', *RES*, xxv (1949), 193-209.

MACKIE, W. S. 'Notes on Old English Poetry', *MLN*, xl (1925), 92-3.

MIDGLEY, GRAHAM. '"The Wanderer", lines 49-55', *RES*, x (1959), 53-4.

OWEN, W. J. B. '*Wanderer*, lines 50-57', *MLN*, lxv (1950), 161-5.

SALMON, VIVIAN. '*The Wanderer* and *The Seafarer*, and the Old English Conception of the Soul', *MLR*, lv (1960), 1-10.

SCHIPPER, J. 'Zum Codex Exoniensis', *Germania*, xix (1874), 327-38.

SCHRÖDER, H. 'Beiträge zur deutschen Wortforschung', *ZfdP*, xxxvii (1905), 393-4.

SHIPLEY, G. *The Genitive Case in Anglo-Saxon Poetry*. Dissertation. Baltimore, 1903.

SMITHERS, G. V. 'Five Notes on Old English Texts', *English and Germanic Studies*, iv (1951-2), 84-85.

STOELKE, H. *Die Inkongruenz zwischen Subjekt und Prädikat im Englischen und in den verwandten Sprachen*, Anglistische Forschungen, 49. Heidelberg, 1916.

STRUNK, W. JR. 'Notes on the shorter Old English Poems', *MLN*, xviii (1903), 72-3.

SUDDABY, ELIZABETH. 'Three Notes on Old English Texts', *MLN*, lxix (1954), 465-6.

TUPPER, F. JR. 'Notes on Old English Poems: V *Hond Ofer Heafod*', *JEGP*, xi (1912), 96-100.

WEMAN, B. *Old English Semantic Analysis and Theory*. Lund, 1933.

WRENN, C. L. 'The Value of Spelling as Evidence', *Transactions of the Philological Society*, 1943, 29-30.

ZUPITZA, J. 'Zu Wanderer 31', *Archiv*, lxxxvi (1890), 279-80.

THEME AND STRUCTURE

BOER, R. C. 'Wanderer und Seefahrer', *ZfdP*, xxxv (1903), 1-28.

BROOKE, S. A. *The History of Early English Literature*, 2 vols. London, 1892.

BROOKE, S. A. *English Literature from the Beginning to the Norman Conquest*. London, 1898.

CHADWICK, H. M. and N. K. *The Growth of Literature*, vol. I. Cambridge, 1932.

CROSS, J. E. 'On *The Wanderer* lines 80-84, a Study of a Figure and a Theme', *Vetenskaps-Societetens i Lund Årsbok*, 1958-9, pp. 77-110.

CROSS, J. E. 'On the Genre of *The Wanderer*', *Neophilologus*, xlv (1961), 63-72.

EHRISMANN, G. 'Religionsgeschichtliche beiträge zum germanischen frühchristentum', *Beiträge*, xxxv (1909), 209-39.

ELLIOTT, R. W. V. 'The Wanderer's Conscience', *English Studies*, xxxix (1958), 193-200.

ERZGRÄBER, WILLI. '*Der Wanderer*. Eine Interpretation von Aufbau und Gehalt', *Festschrift zum 75. Geburtstag von Theodor Spira* (Heidelberg, 1961), pp. 57-85.

FERRELL, C. C. 'Old Germanic Life in the Anglo-Saxon "Wanderer" and "Seafarer"', *MLN*, ix (1894), 402-7.

GORDON, IDA L. 'Traditional Themes in *The Wanderer* and *The Seafarer*', *RES*, v (1954), 1-13.

GREENFIELD, S. B. '*The Wanderer*: A Reconsideration of Theme and Structure', *JEGP*, l (1951), 451-65.

GREENFIELD, S. B. 'The Formulaic Expression of the Theme of "Exile" in Anglo-Saxon Poetry', *Speculum*, xxx (1955), 200-6.

GRUBL, EMILY D. *Studien zu den angelsächsischen Elegien.* Marburg, 1948.

HEUSLER, A. 'Der Dialog in der altgermanischen erzählenden Dichtung', *ZfdA*, xlvi (1902), 189-284.

HEUSLER, A. Review of Imelmann's *Forschungen zur Altenglischen Poesie* in *AfdA*, xli (1922), 27-31.

HEUSLER, A. *Die Altgermanische Dichtung.* Berlin, 1923.

HUPPÉ, B. F. 'The Wanderer: Theme and Structure', *JEGP*, xlii (1943), 516-38.

IDELMANN, THEODORA. *Das Gefühl in den altenglischen Elegien.* Dissertation. Münster, 1932.

KENNEDY, C. W. *The Earliest English Poetry.* New York, 1943.

KLUGE, F. 'Zu altenglischen Dichtungen, I', *Englische Studien*, vi (1883), 322-7.

KÖRTING, G. *Grundriss der Geschichte der Englischen Literatur.* Second edition. Münster, 1893.

LAWRENCE, W. W. 'The Wanderer and the Seafarer', *JGP*, iv (1902), 460-80. [Published after Boer's article in *ZfdP*, vol. xxxv.]

LUMIANSKY, R. M. 'The Dramatic Structure of the Old English *Wanderer*', *Neophilologus*, xxxiv (1950), 104-12.

MALONE, K. and BAUGH, A. C. *The Middle Ages.* New York, 1948.

MORLEY, H. *English Writers*, vol. II. London, 1888.

POPE, J. C. 'Dramatic Voices in *The Wanderer* and *The Seafarer*', *Franciplegius: Medieval and Linguistic Studies in Honor of Francis Peabody Magoun Jr.* (New York, 1965), pp. 164-93.

PRINS, A. A. 'The Wanderer (and the Seafarer)', *Neophilologus*, xlviii (1964), 237-51.

RIEGER, M. 'Über Cynewulf V', *ZfdP*, i (1869), 324-39.

ROBERTSON, D. W. JR. 'Historical Criticism', *English Institute Essays*, 1950, New York, 1951, pp. 17-23.

ROSIER, JAMES L. 'The Literal-Figurative Identity of *The Wanderer*', *PMLA*, lxxix (1964), 366-9.

ROSTEUTSCHER, J. H. W. 'Germanischer Schicksalsglaube und angelsächsische Elegiendichtung', *Englische Studien*, lxxiii (1938), 1-31.

RUMBLE, T. C. 'From *Eardstapa* to *Snottor on mode*: The Structural Principle of "The Wanderer"', *MLQ*, xix (1958), 225-30.

SCHÜCKING, L. L. 'Wann Entstand der Beowulf?', *Beiträge*, xlii (1917), 388-410.

SCHÜCKING, L. L. Review of Sieper's *Die Altenglische Elegie* in *Englische Studien* li (1917-18), 97-115.

SMITHERS, G. V. 'The Meaning of *The Seafarer* and *The Wanderer*', *Medium Aevum*, xxvi (1957), 137-53.

SMITHERS, G. V. 'The Meaning of *The Seafarer* and *The Wanderer* (continued)', *Medium Aevum* xxviii (1959), 1-22.

STANLEY, E. G. 'Old English Poetic Diction and the Interpretation of *The Wanderer*, *The Seafarer* and *The Penitent's Prayer*', *Anglia*, lxxiii (1955), 413-66.

TEN BRINK, B. *Geschichte der Englischen Litteratur* I. Second edition. Berlin, 1899.

TIMMER, B. J. '*Wyrd* in Anglo-Saxon Prose and Poetry', *Neophilologus*, xxvi (1941), 24-33, 213-28.

TIMMER, B. J. 'The Elegiac Mood in Old English Poetry', *English Studies*, xxiv (1942), 33-44. In the same volume, 'Irony in Old English', pp. 171-5.

TIMMER, B. J. 'Heathen and Christian Elements in Old English Poetry', *Neophilologus*, xxix (1944), 180-5.

TRENEER, ANNE. *The Sea in English Literature*. Liverpool, 1922.

TUCKER, S. I. 'Return to *The Wanderer*', *Essays in Criticism*, viii (1958), 229-37.

WARDALE, E. E. *Chapters on Old English Literature*. London, 1935.

WILLIAMS, BLANCHE C. *Gnomic Poetry in Anglo-Saxon*. New York, 1914.

WÜLKER, R. *Grundriss zur Geschichte der angelsächsischen Litteratur*. Leipzig, 1885.

HISTORICAL AND LITERARY BACKGROUND

ANDERSON, G. K. *The Literature of the Anglo-Saxons*. Oxford, 1949.

BARTLETT, A. C. *The Larger Rhetorical Patterns in Anglo-Saxon Poetry*. New York, 1935.

BECKER, C. H. 'Ubi sunt qui ante nos in mundo fuere', *Aufsätze zur Kultur- und Sprachgeschichte, vornehmlich des Orients*, Ernst Kuhn zum siebzigsten Geburtstage gewidmet. Breslau, 1916, pp. 87-105.

BETHURUM, DOROTHY (editor), *Critical Approaches to Medieval Literature*. Selected Papers from The English Institute, 1958-9. New York, 1960.

BISCHOFF, B. 'Wendepunkte in der Geschichte der lateinischen Exegese im Frühmittelalter', *Sacris Erudiri*, vi (1954), 189-281.

BLOOMFIELD, MORTON W. 'Symbolism in Medieval Literature', *Modern Philology*, lvi (1958), 73-81.

BRANDL, A. 'Venantius Fortunatus und die angelsächsischen Elegien "Wanderer" und "Ruine"', *Archiv*, cxxxix (1919), 84.

BRIGHT, J. W. 'The *ubi sunt* Formula', *MLN*, viii (1893), 187-8.

CHADWICK, H. M. 'Early National Poetry', *Cambridge History of English Literature*, vol. I. Cambridge, 1907, pp. 37-9.

CHADWICK, NORA K. 'The Celtic West', *The Heritage of Early Britain* (London, 1952), pp. 104-27.

CHADWICK, NORA K. *Poetry and Letters in early Christian Gaul*. London, 1955.

CHADWICK, NORA K. 'The Celtic Background of Early Anglo-Saxon England', *Celt and Saxon: Studies in the Early British Border* (Cambridge, 1963), pp. 323-52.

CHANEY, WILLIAM A. 'Paganism to Christianity in Anglo-Saxon England', *Harvard Theological Review*, liii (1960), 197-217.

CROSS, J. E. '"Ubi Sunt" Passages in Old English—Sources and Relationships', *Vetenskaps-Societetens i Lund Årsbok*, 1956, pp. 25-44.

CROSS, J. E. 'Aspects of Microcosm and Macrocosm in Old English Literature', *Comparative Literature*, xiv (1962), 1-22.

DUNLEAVY, G. W. *Colum's Other Island: The Irish at Lindisfarne*. University of Wisconsin Press. Madison, 1960, pp. 78-92.

ELLIOTT, R. W. V. 'Form and Image in Old English Lyrics', *Essays in Criticism*, xi (1961), 1-9.

GÖLLER, KARL H. 'Die angelsächsischen Elegien', *Germanisch-Romanische Monatsschrift*, xlv (1964), 225-41.

GORDON, IDA L. *The Seafarer*. London, 1960.

HUPPÉ, BERNARD F. *Doctrine and Poetry*. Albany, 1959.

JACKSON, K. *Studies in Early Celtic Nature Poetry*. Cambridge, 1935.

KASKE, R. E. '*Sapientia et Fortitudo* as the Controlling Theme of *Beowulf*', *Studies in Philology*, lv (1958), 423-56.

KEISER, A. *The Influence of Christianity on the Vocabulary of Old English Poetry*, reprinted from *University of Illinois Studies in Language and Literature*, V. Illinois, 1919.

KLAEBER, F. 'Aeneis und Beowulf', *Archiv*, cxxvi (1911), **339-59**.

LAISTNER, M. L. W. *Thought and Letters in Western Europe, A.D. 500-900.* Second edition. London, 1957.

LEONARD, H. FREY. 'Exile and Elegy in Anglo-Saxon Christian Epic Poetry', *JEGP*, lxii (1963), 293-302.

LEVISON, W. *England and the Continent in the Eighth Century.* Oxford, 1946.

MAGOUN, F. P. JR. 'Oral-Formulaic Character of Anglo-Saxon Narrative Poetry', *Speculum*, xxviii (1953), 446-67.

MEYER, KUNO. *The Instructions of King Cormac MacAirt.* Royal Irish Academy, Todd Lectures Series, xv. Dublin, 1909.

O'NEIL, W. A. *Oral-Formulaic Structure in Old English Elegiac Poetry.* Unpublished Doctoral Dissertation. University of Wisconsin, 1960. [Abstract in *Dissertation Abstracts* xxi (1960), 625.]

PILCH, HERBERT. 'The Elegiac Genre in Old English and Early Welsh Poetry', *Zeitschrift für Celtische Philologie*, xxix (1964), 209-24.

PONS, E. *Le Thème et le Sentiment de la Nature dans la Poesie Anglo-Saxonne.* Strasbourg, 1925.

REUSCHEL, HELGA. 'Ovid und die Ags. Elegien', *Beiträge*, lxii (1938), 132-42.

SCHÜCKING, L. L. 'Das angelsächsische Totenklagelied', *Englische Studien*, xxxix (1908), 1-13.

STEVICK, ROBERT D. 'The Oral-Formulaic Analyses of Old English Verse', *Speculum*, xxxvii (1962), 382-9.

TURVILLE-PETRE, JOAN. 'Translations of a Lost Penitential Homily', *Traditio*, xix (1963), 51-78.

WHITMAN, C. H. 'The Birds of Old English Literature', *JGP*, ii (1898), 149-98.

WRENN, C. L. 'Saxons and Celts in South-West Britain', *Transactions of the Honourable Society of Cymmrodorion* (London, 1959), pp. 38-75.

LANGUAGE

ANDREW, S. O. *Syntax and Style in Old English.* Cambridge, **1940.**

BROOK, G. L. 'The Relation between the Textual and the Linguistic Study of Old English', *The Anglo-Saxons, Studies in some Aspects of their History and Culture* presented to Bruce Dickins (London, 1959), pp. 280-91.

BRUNNER, K. *Altenglische Grammatik nach der Angelsächsischen Grammatik von E. Sievers.* Second edition. Halle, 1951.

CAMPBELL, A. *Old English Grammar.* Oxford, 1959.

MARQUARDT, HERTHA. *Die Altenglischen Kenningar, Ein Beitrag zur Stilkunde altgermanischer Dichtung.* Halle, 1938.

SISAM, K. 'Dialect Origins of the Earlier Old English Verse', *Studies in the History of Old English Literature,* pp. 119-39. Oxford, 1953.

SUPPLEMENTARY BIBLIOGRAPHY

ANTHONY, MOTHER MARY. 'Aesthetic Balance in *The Wanderer*', *LHR*, viii (1966), 1–7.

BESSAI, FRANK. 'Comitatus and Exile in Old English Poetry', *Culture*, vi (1964), 130-4.

BURROW, JOHN. '*The Wanderer:* Lines 73-87', *Notes and Queries,* May 1965, xii (N.S.), 166-8.

CAMPBELL, J. J. and JAMES L. ROSIER (eds.). *Poems in Old English.* New York, 1962.

CROSSLEY-HOLLAND, KEVIN (translator) and BRUCE MITCHELL (ed.). *The Battle of Maldon and other Old English Poems.* London, 1965.

DEAN, CHRISTOPHER. '*Weal Wundrum Heah, Wyrmlicum Fah* and the Narrative Background of *The Wanderer*', *Modern Philology*, lxiii (1965), 141-3.

DUNLEAVY, GARETH W. *Colum's Other Island.* Madison, 1960.

GOTTLIEB, STEPHEN A. 'The Metaphors of *Wanderer* Lines 53a-55a', *NM*, lxvi (1965), 145-8.

LEE, ALVIN A. 'From Grendel to the *Phoenix:* A Critical Study of Old English Elegiac Poetry.' Toronto Dissertation, 1961.

MITCHELL, BRUCE. 'Some Problems of Mood and Tense in Old English', *Neophilologus*, xliv (1965), 44-6.

THE WANDERER

Note on the Text

THE text of the present edition was transcribed from the facsimile of the *Exeter Book* and afterwards collated with the manuscript. Square brackets are used to indicate letters supplied by the editor either in place of the MS. reading or in addition to it.

All the MS. abbreviations are expanded without notice. The most consistently used abbreviation is 7 for *ond*; þon̄ and ðon̄ for *þonne* and *ðonne* are used for eight out of nine occurrences of the word. Occasional use is made of þ̄ for *þæt* and of the abbreviation mark for a nasal above a vowel. There is only one accent, over the *a* on *nan* (9), a vowel which is etymologically long.

f. 76b

'Oft him ānhaga   āre gebīdeð,
Metudes miltse,   þeahþe hē mōdcearig
geond lagulāde   longe sceolde
hrēran mid hondum   hrīmcealde sǣ,
5 wadan wræclāstas;   wyrd bið ful ārǣd.'
  Swā cwæð eardstapa   earfeþa gemyndig,
wrāþra wælsleahta,   winemǣga hryre.
  'Oft ic sceolde āna   ūhtna gehwylce
mīne ceare cwīþan;   nis nū cwicra nān
10 þe ic him mōdsefan   mīnne durre
sweotule āsecgan.   Ic tō sōþe wāt
þæt biþ in eorle   indryhtcn þēaw
þæt hē his ferðlocan   fæste binde,
healde his hordcofan,   hycge swā hē wille.
15 Ne mæg wērigmōd   wyrde wiðstondan
ne sē hrēo hyge   helpe gefremman.
Forðon dōmgeorne   drēorigne oft
in hyra brēostcofan   bindað fæste.
Swā ic mōdsefan   mīnne sceolde,
20 oft earmcearig,   ēðle bidǣled,
frēomǣgum feor   feterum sǣlan,
siþþan geāra iū   goldwine mīn[n]e
hrūsan heolstre biwrāh,   ond ic hēan þonan
wōd wintercearig   ofer waþe[m]a gebind,
25 sōhte seledrēorig   sinces bryttan,
hwǣr ic feor oþþe nēah   findan meahte,
þone þe in meoduhealle   [mē] mine wisse
oþþe mec frēondlēas[n]e   frēfran wolde,
wēman mid wynnum.
                Wāt sē þe cunnað

14 healde: *MS.* healdne   22 mīnne: *MS.* mine
24 waþema: *MS.* waþena   27 mē *not in MS.*
28 frēondlēasne: *MS.* freond lease

30 hū slīþen bið   sorg tō gefēran

þām þe him lȳt hafað   lēofra geholena;

warað hine wræclāst   nāles wunden gold,

f. 77a   ferðloca frēorig   nālæs foldan blǣd.

Gemon hē selesecgas   ond sincþege,

35 hū hine on geoguðe   his goldwine

wenede tō wiste;   wyn eal gedrēas.

Forþon wāt sē þe sceal   his winedryhtnes

lēofes lārcwidum   longe forþolian,

ðonne sorg ond slǣp   somod ætgædre

40 earmne ānhogan   oft gebindað,

þinceð him on mōde   þæt hē his mondryhten

clyppe ond cysse   ond on cnēo lecge

honda ond hēafod   swā hē hwīlum ǣr

in geārdagum   giefstōlas brēac.

45 Ðonne onwæcneð eft   winelēas guma,

gesihð him biforan   fealwe wēgas,

baþian brimfuglas   brǣdan feþra,

hrēosan hrīm ond snāw   hagle gemenged.

Þonne bēoð þȳ hefigran   heortan benne,

50 sāre æfter swǣsne.   Sorg bið genīwad

þonne māga gemynd   mōd geondhweorfeð,

grēteð glīwstafum,   georne geondscēawað

secga geseldan—swimmað oft onweg

flēotendra ferð—nō þǣr fela bringeð

55 cūðra cwidegiedda.   Cearo bið genīwad

þām þe sendan sceal   swīþe geneahhe

ofer waþema gebind   wērigne sefan.

Forþon ic geþencan ne mæg   geond þās woruld

for hwan mōdsefa   mīn ne gesweorce

60 þonne ic eorla līf   eal geondþence,

hū hī fǣrlīce   flet ofgēafon,

mōdge maguþegnas.   Swā þes middangeard

ealra dōgra gehwām   drēoseð ond fealleþ.

Forþon ne mæg wearþan wīs   wer ǣr hē āge

59 mōdsefa mīn ne: *MS.* mod sefan minne

f. 77b 65 wintra dǣl in woruldrīce. Wita sceal geþyldig;
ne sceal nō tō hātheort   ne tō hrædwyrde,
ne tō wāc wiga   ne tō wanhȳdig,
ne tō forht, ne tō fǣgen,   ne tō feohgīfre,
ne nǣfre gielpes tō georn   ǣr hē geare cunne.
70 Beorn sceal gebīdan   þonne hē bēot spriceð
oþþæt collenferð   cunne gearwe
hwider hreþra gehygd   hweorfan wille.
   Ongietan sceal glēaw hǣle   hū gǣstlic bið
þonne eall þisse worulde wela   wēste stondeð,
75 swā nū missenlīce   geond þisne middangeard
winde biwāune   weallas stondaþ,
hrīme bihrorene,   hrȳðge þā ederas.
Wōriað þā wīnsalo,   waldend licgað
drēame bidrorene;   duguþ eal gecrong
80 wlonc bī wealle. Sume wīg fornōm,
ferede in forðwege;   sumne fugel oþbær
ofer hēanne holm;   sumne sē hāra wulf
dēaðe gedǣlde;   sumne drēorighlēor
in eorðscræfe   eorl gehȳdde.
85 Ȳþde swā þisne eardgeard   ælda Scyppend
oþþæt burgwara   breahtma lēase
eald enta geweorc   īdlu stōdon.
   Sē þonne þisne wealsteal   wīse geþōhte
ond þis deorce līf   dēope geondþenceð
90 frōd in ferðe,   feor oft gemon
wælsleahta worn   ond þās word ācwið:
   "Hwǣr cwōm mearg? Hwǣr cwōm mago?
                     Hwǣr cwōm maþþumgyfa?
Hwǣr cwōm symbla gesetu? Hwǣr sindon sele-
      drēamas?
Ēalā beorht būne! Ēalā byrnwiga!
95 Ēalā þēodnes þrym! Hū sēo þrāg gewāt,
genāp under nihthelm   swā hēo nō wǣre."
   Stondeð nū on lāste   lēofre duguþe

74 eall: *MS.* ealle   89 deorce: *MS.* deornce

78a   weal wundrum hēah   wyrmlīcum fāh.

      Eorlas fornōman   asca þrȳþe,

100 wǣpen wælgīfru,   wyrd sēo mǣre;

      ond þās stānhleoþu   stormas cnyssað;

      hrīð hrēosende   hrūs[an] bindeð,

      wintres wōma;   þonne won cymeð

      nīpeð nihtscūa   norþan onsendeð

105 hrēo hæglfare   hæleþum on andan.

      Eall is earfoðlic   eorþan rīce;

      onwendeð wyrda gesceaft   weoruld under

         heofonum.

      Hēr bið feoh lǣne,   hēr bið frēond lǣne,

      hēr bið mon lǣne,   hēr bið mǣg lǣne.

110 Eal þis eorþan gesteal   īdel weorþeð.'

       Swā cwæð snottor on mōde;   gesæt him sundor

         æt rūne.

      ' Til biþ sē þe his trēowe gehealdeþ,   ne sceal nǣfre

         his torn tō rycene,

      beorn of his brēostum ācȳþan   nemþe hē ǣr þā

         bōte cunne;

      eorl mid elne gefremman.   Wel bið þām þe him āre

         sēceð,

115 frōfre tō Fæder on heofonum,   þǣr ūs eal sēo

         fæstnung stondeð.'

100 e *in* mǣre *is altered from* o
102 hrūsan: *MS.* hruse

NOTES

1. **ānhaga** is glossed ' einsiedler ', namely ' recluse ', by Holthausen (*Altenglisches Etymologisches Wörterbuch*, p. 147, *haga* 2), who derives it from *ān* and *haga* ' dwelling, enclosure '. The compound occurs in a number of Old English poems containing exile or outcast imagery. Discussion of its etymology is complicated by the occurrence in similar contexts of a form with *o* in the stem, as in line 40 of *The Wanderer: earmne ānhogan*, and in *Guthlac* 997, *The Phoenix* 346, *Resignation* 89 and the metrical hymn 4.88. Mrs. Ida L. Gordon in ' Traditional Themes in *The Wanderer* and *The Seafarer* ', *RES*, v (1954), 3, translates *ānhaga* as ' one who meditates alone ' and connects it with *hogian* ' to think ' rather than *haga* ' enclosure ', since weak masculine nouns normally denote active agents, so that *haga* is properly ' that which encloses '. There is no great difficulty, however, if *haga* is assumed to have developed early the meaning ' place, dwelling ' alongside the basic sense ' enclosure, fence ', like the semantically similar place-name elements *tūn* and *burg*, which developed in this way; *ānhaga*, literally ' one who dwells alone ', is likely therefore to have been derived from *haga* in the sense of ' dwelling '. Certainly the contexts of both the *-haga* and the *-hoga* forms suggest similarity of meaning (cf. especially *The Phoenix* 87 and 346), but the *a* of *ānhaga* is difficult to account for on the assumption of derivation from *hogian*. The Latin gloss to which Mrs. Gordon has drawn attention gives *solitarius* for *ānhoga oððe ānwuniende* (Lambeth Psalter 101.8), a meaning which suggests derivation from *haga* ' dwelling ' rather than *hoga* ' one who meditates '. Possibly the forms are to be regarded as ablaut variants, like *gehola* and *gehala*, *gafol* and *gofol*, or *morgen* and *margen*; but whereas these go back to Indo-European forms with secondary and vanishing grades, the relationship between *haga* and *hoga* is likely to have been a more complex one of lengthened and normal grades of *a* (cf. Latin *caulae*). Alternatively, two words *ānhaga* and *ānhoga* may have been coined separately, and the Germanic conception of solitude as a state of care and anxiety may then have led to confusion in their use.

That *āre* means ' mercy ' here is indicated by the variant *miltse* (2). In *Runic Poem* 19-21: (*gyfu*) . . . *bið* . . . *wræcna gehwām/ār and ætwist*, there is a similar association with exile-wanderers.

gebīdeð. The sense ' experiences ' rather than ' awaits ' or ' expects ' is to be preferred here, because the prefix *ge-* denotes completion and the adverbial clause beginning *þēahþe* ' even though ' implies fulfilment rather than expectation in the verb *gebīdeð*; cf. the similar meaning of this verb in *Beowulf* 1060b-1062:

Fela sceal gebīdan
lēofes ond lāþes   sē þe longe hēr
on ðyssum windagum   worolde brūceð!

Cf. Timmer, *Neophilologus*, xxvi. 221 and Greenfield, *JEGP*, 1. 464-5. Erzgräber's conclusion (*loc. cit.* pp. 77-8) that this interpretation of *gebīdeð* points clearly to the utterance of these lines, not by the wanderer, but by the poet in his own voice, is not so certain as he claims, for it depends entirely on our acceptance of a wanderer who remains unconsoled while he utters his monologue.

4: hrīmcealde is an adjective which does not appear elsewhere in OE, although the corresponding form *hrímkaldr* occurs three times in ON poetry, where it applies to supernatural beings (cf. N. Kershaw, *Anglo-Saxon and Norse Poems*, p. 162); but a similar compound *īsceald* occurs in *The Seafarer* 14, 19, and in *The Metres of Boethius* 27. 2-4: *swā swā mereflōdes/ȳþa hrērað īscalde sǣ,/wecggað for winde*, a passage which also illustrates the significance of *hrēran*.

5. wadan wræclāstas. The same phrase also constitutes a first half-line in *Christ and Satan* 120.

Interpretation of **ārǣd** as the reduced form of the past participle of *ārǣdan* 'determine' was suggested by Sedgefield; cf. also Klaeber, *Anglia Beiblatt*, xl. 30. Support for such an interpretation appears to be supplied by *Maxims* I, 191: *geāra is hwǣr ārǣd.* **Wyrd** appears to have here the passive sense of a man's lot, as suggested by Timmer, *Neophilologus*, xxvi. 221; cf. *Beowulf* 455: *Gǣð ā wyrd swā hīo scel.* The poet may also have had in mind Boethius' concept of *fatum* subject to the dominion of *providentia*, in Book IV, Prosa 6 of his *De Consolatione Philosophiae*; cf. Erzgräber, *loc. cit.* pp. 77-9. K. H. Göller (*Germanisch-Romanische Monatsschrift*, xlv. 237) perceives still 'das starre Gesicht der alten Norne hinter dem unpersönlichen Begriff'. God is frequently depicted in Anglo-Saxon poetry as the ruler of *wyrd*; cf. R. J. Menner, *The Poetical Dialogues of Solomon and Saturn* (New York, 1941), pp. 62-3. Reconciliation of the intervention of God in lines 1 and 2 with a pre-ordained course of events is thus made easier. Erzgräber's suggestion that line 5b be made part of a second clause introduced by *þēahþe* makes the relationship between the two concepts clearer, but somewhat detracts from the force of the statement; it seems preferable to regard it as parenthetic.

6. eardstapa. Most compounds of *-stapa* in Old English poetry refer to animals, the first element denoting the habitat of the creature; cf. the reference to Grendel as a *mearcstapa* in *Beowulf* 103. *Eardstapa*, a unique compound, is appropriately to be taken therefore as one whose habitat is the whole land. It may be by this choice of word that the poet places his protagonist with those beings which live away from the homes of men.

6-7. Here the credentials'of the wanderer appear to be formally presented; cf. the introduction of Sigeferþ in *The Finnsburg Fragment* 24-6: *Ic eom Secgena lēod,/wreccea wīde cūð; fæla ic wēana gebād,/heordra hilda.*

7. **winemǣga hryre.** In place of MS. *hryre* we should expect after *gemyndig* a genitive form *hryres*, in apposition to *earfeþa* (6) and *wælsleahta* (7). In *Darstellung der syntaktischen Erscheinungen im angelsächsischen Gedichte vom Wanderer*, p. 82, Jacobsen seeks to justify *hryre* as an accusative; Miss Kershaw describes it as a loose comitative instrumental. Neither suggestion seems convincing in view of the twenty-six occurrences elsewhere in poetry of *gemyndig* followed by a noun in the genitive. Fischer (*Anglia*, lix. 301) takes *hryre* as accusative after *cwæð* meaning ' announced ' and Kock (*Jubilee Jaunts and Jottings*, p. 78) takes *winemǣga hryre* as the opening of a new sentence, with *hryre* the object of *cwīþan* (9), parallel to *mīne ceare*; the weakness of both solutions is that they require acceptance of unusual and unidiomatic word order. More acceptable is Toller's citation of *hryre* as a dative after *gemyndig*, on the basis of the occurrence of such a construction in Ælfric's Homilies (Thorpe's edition, I, p. 312, line 34). Emendation of *hryre* to *hryres* is best avoided, because of the possibility that it is a dative after *gemyndig*, despite the genitive constructions which precede it, and because in at least sixteen occurrences in Old English poetry of *hryre* with a dependent genitive, *hryre* is invariably the form, either as a nominative or accusative singular, or, most frequently, as a dative singular. Since the familiar stereotype in the oblique case is therefore the dative singular *hryre*, it seems likely that this analogy prevailed; failure to make the alteration to *hryres* in the context of *The Wanderer* could have been facilitated by the distance of the phrase *winemǣga hryre* from the adjective *gemyndig* on which it might be expected to depend in the genitive.

8-9. *Ūhte* is habitually used with precision of the period just before dawn as shown by the gloss to *valde mane* in Mark 16.2 and in Alfred's translation of Gregory's *Pastoral Care* (Sweet's edition, p. 461, line 2), where *ūhtan* translates *profundioribus horis noctis.* Dawn itself is indicated by *dægrēd*; cf. *on ūhtan . . . ǣr dægrēde* in *Christ and Satan* 463-4. Early morning appears to have been a time of special misery, as shown in *Beowulf* 129, 2007, 3021-2, *Resignation* 96, and *The Wife's Lament* 7, 35-8; cf. also E. G. Stanley, *Anglia*, lxxiii. 434-5.

10. The rule, whereby the third person pronoun immediately follows the relative particle *þe*, does not appear to apply here because the subject of the relative clause is a pronoun, namely *ic*, which is independent of the relative combination (see Bruce Mitchell, *RES*, xv (1964), 136); cf. the similar syntactical order in *Elene*, 162: *þe þis his bēacen was.*

12. **indryhten.** The prefix *in-* of this adjective is probably the intensifier meaning ' very ' which is found in a number of Old English

adjectives, such as *infrōd* and *inhold*. This intensifier is generally added to words also current as adjectives in their simple forms; although *dryhten* by itself does not appear to have been in common use as an adjective in Old English, unlike *frōd* and *hold*, the forms *drihtenum* and *drihtnum* before *Gode* and *Criste* (see Toller, *dryhten* adj.) clearly indicate adjectival use in the dative singular. Possibly its use in the simplex form was inhibited by the frequent occurrence of the noun *dryhten* in which *-en* is part of the stem, whereas the *-en* of the adjective is from the Germanic adjectival ending *-īna*. *Indryhten* occurs only twice elsewhere, in *Riddles* 43.1 and 95.1.

13. ferðloca is the most frequent compound of *fer(h)ð* in Old English poetry and is particularly common with *fæste*; cf. *Juliana* 234 and *Andreas* 58, 1671.

13-14. These sentiments are closely associated in similar contexts in Old English poetry; cf. *Precepts* 57-8, *Maxims* I, 121, and *Homiletic Fragment* II, 3-4 where the phrasing is very similar: *heald hordlocan, hyge fæste binde,/mid mōdsefan*. *Hordcofan* occurs only here and in the metrical *Psalm* 118.2; cf. the much more familiar *-cofa* compound *brēostcofan* in line 18.

14. healde as an emendation of MS. *healdne* was first suggested by Thorpe and has been adopted by most editors. Grein retains *healdne* and describes it as an accusative, but does not explain it. The form could be interpreted as the masculine accusative singular of an adjective *heald* 'bent, inclined', but such an interpretation would be both semantically and syntactically inappropriate here. On the other hand, the parallelism of *ferðlocan . . . binde* and *healde . . . hordcofan* after the conjunction *þæt* is a strong argument for reading *healde*, the third person singular present subjunctive of *healdan*.

16. The semantic range of *hrēo* in Old English is wide, going from 'rough, cruel' through 'troubled' to 'sad'. Elliott (*English Studies*, xxxix. 194) reminds us that it is cognate with the noun *hrēoh* 'stormy weather'; but it may also be cognate with *hrēow* 'grief'. Elliott's emphasis on ferocity to support his picture of a conscience-stricken wanderer accords ill with the prevalent tone of the other adjectives in this part of the poem, and especially with *drēorigne* in the following line, which probably qualifies *hyge*, understood from the previous line.

This line varies the preceding one so that *helpe gefremman* is parallel with *wyrde wiðstondan*. Whereas these lines indicate that a man cannot find help within himself, the phrase *helpe gefremman* is used in *Andreas* 425-6 to point out that God can easily bring help to seafarers.

17. The *dōmgeorne* are those eager to leave a reputation behind them. According to *Maxims* I, 139-40, a man must *lofes gearnian,/dōm āreccan*. *Dōm* is the considered judgment of others; cf. *Hávamál*, stanza 77. The linking of fame with taciturnity is directly echoed in *Homiletic*

Fragment II, 2-3; *þinne dōm ārær,/heald hordlocan, hyge fæste bind.* Miss Kershaw is uncertain whether reserve or caution is intended. The use of *durre* in line 10 and the injunction in similar circumstances in *Precepts* 57-8:

> Wærwyrde sceal   wīsfæst hæle
> brēostum hycgan, nāles breahtme hlūd.

suggest that the motive for taciturnity is caution.

drēorigne. The context indicates that a noun such as *mōd* or *hyge* is required for *drēorigne* to qualify; the masculine noun *hyge* is probably to be understood from the previous line. Craigie assumes a word missing after *oft*; but the half-line is metrically complete and can be scanned as type E. *Oft* can take a full stress as in *Beowulf* 2500 and 2937, and the suffix of *drēorig* can carry secondary stress as indicated by the metrically similar half-line *drīorigne fand* (*Beowulf* 2789b).

19. *Swā* introduces here an individual exemplification of the preceding general observation, as in *Beowulf* 1769 and 3066.

20. **earmcearig** occurs only here and in *The Seafarer* 14. As Anderson has shown, other compounds of *-cearig*, such as *hrēowcearig*, *sorgcearig* and *gnorncearig*, have nouns as their first elements. In compounds consisting of two adjectival elements in *The Gifts of Men*, the first apparently qualifies the second; e.g. *læthȳdig* (10), *hēanspēdig* (26), *wonspēdig* (31), and *heardsǣlig* (32). *Earmcearig* may be taken to mean 'wretched with care'.

22. Most editors emend MS. *mine* to *minne*. Thorpe's assumption that a scribe had omitted an abbreviation mark over *n* is a probable explanation of the absence of an *n*; the omission may have been facilitated by the influence of *-ine* in the preceding *wine*. Grein-Wülker keep the MS. reading as a poetic plural; but cf. the unambiguously singular *goldwine* in line 35.

23. **hrūsan heolstre** has frequently been emended unnecessarily. We may with Kock (*Anglia*, xxvii. 227) take, as the subject of *biwrāh*, *ic* understood from the previous lines, as it is in line 25; cf. *Beowulf* 470. *Heolstre* is the instrumental of the well-attested noun *heolstor*, with *hrūsan* dependent upon it in the genitive: 'I concealed my lord in the darkness of the earth'; cf. *heolstre behȳded* (*Elene* 1081) of the nails of the cross.

hēan is interpreted by Elliott (*English Studies*, xxxix. 195-6) as 'disgraced, humiliated', but the basic meaning is 'abject' and any pejorative sense is given by the context, e.g. Adam confronted by God in *Genesis* 866, 879. When, as in *The Wanderer*, the adjective is part of a stereotyped exile image, namely *hēan* followed by an adjective denoting sadness and a verb of departure, the basic meaning is predominant; cf. Greenfield ' The Formulaic Expression of the Theme of

" Exile " in Anglo-Saxon Poetry ', *Speculum* xxx (1955), 200-6. In a similar passage in *Guthlac*, it is said of a man who has just lost his lord: *Hē sceal hēan þonan,/geōmor hweorfan* (1353-4); here there is no doubt about the retainer's integrity, and there need be no doubt about the wanderer's, unless clear evidence to the contrary were to be shown elsewhere.

24. wintercearig occurs uniquely here and is the third in a series of -*cearig* compounds in the poem, the other two being *mōdcearig* (2) and *earmcearig* (20). The first element may refer to the season or to old age. Bosworth-Toller cite lines 34-6 in support of the latter; but *wintercearig* refers not to his present state of mind but to his feelings long ago, *geāra iū* (22), as he left his lord's grave. The adjective should probably be taken to mean desolate with the desolation of winter, an intimate blend of personal wretchedness with a harsh environment, which is notable throughout the poem; cf. *wintercald* and *winterbiter*.

ofer waþema gebind. The occurrence of the same phrase in line 57a supports the emendation of *n* to *m* in MS. *wapena*. *Gebind* is held by Sweet and Gollancz to refer to frozen waves, but in the same phrase in line 57 the *waþema gebind* over which the lonely voyager travels is the *fealwe wēgas* in which he has just seen the seabirds bathing. A more likely sense for *gebind* is ' expanse '; cf. O.E.D. *bind* 6, where it is pointed out that the word is used provincially to denote a large quantity of anything.

25. seledrēorig is often printed as two words; *drēorig* is taken as a nominative singular adjective qualifying *ic* understood, the subject of *sōhte*; the object of the verb is *sele*, on which *sinces bryttan* depends in the genitive. But the separation of object adjunct from the object by a subject adjunct gives unsatisfactory word-order. Moreover, the metrical pattern of *sōhte sele drēorig* appears excessive, with both over-weighting and extension of a Da type half-line. Adoption of *seledrēorig* gives a unique compound, but is in accordance with the poet's readiness to use compound adjectives of suffering or longing, including the unique form *wintercearig* in the preceding line and the rare one *earmcearig* in line 20. For the meaning ' sad at the loss of the hall ', cf. the analogous formation *winegeōmor* (*Beowulf* 2239) ' sad at the loss of friends '.

26. feor oþþe nēah. The combination of these adverbs in a stereotyped phrase is to be found in another elegiac poem, *The Wife's Lament*, line 25, and also in *Juliana* 335, where they modify a part of the verb *findan*.

27. mē mine wisse. The MS. *mine wisse* is metrically deficient and the sense appears to be incomplete. Thorpe has been followed by many in reading *mine* as a pronoun and assuming that a word had been lost or was to be understood before or after it. Bosworth-Toller (*myne* III) took *mine* as a noun meaning ' love '. Klaeber (*JEGP*, viii. 254) equated it with *myne* in *Beowulf* 169, suggested the meaning ' favour ' and restored *mīn* before *mine*. The verb *wisse* is the third person singular preterite subjunctive of *witan* with the well-attested sense ' feel ' (Bosworth-Toller, *witan* III). Krapp-Dobbie claim that the meanings ' thought, remembrance ' are possible for OE *mine/myne*, but that ' favour, love ' are not authenticated; but in the compound *wīfmyne* (*Genesis* 1861) the meaning ' love ' appears to be clearly attested. Klaeber's restoration *mīn* is open to objection both on syntactical and on metrical grounds. Where *witan* means ' to feel, show ', the person to whom the feeling is shown is regularly put in the dative; *mē* would, therefore, appear to be a better restoration. Moreover, *mīn* carries full stress and alliteration when it is the genitive case of the pronoun initially in a second half-line; cf. *Beowulf* 2084, 2533, *Elene* 347, *Juliana* 521. Since the half-line already has *mine* to alliterate with *meoduhealle* in the first half-line, *mīn* would introduce the rare feature of double alliteration in the second half of a line; *mē* in this position does not carry alliteration or stress, and we can read the half-line as a type C with resolution of the first main stress.

28. **frēondlēasne** has been accepted by all editors since Thorpe suggested it as an emendation of MS. *freond lease* to give agreement with *mec*.

29. **wēman.** A frequent editorial reading is *wenian*, but the MS. clearly has *weman*. Gollancz and Miss Kershaw emend to the near-synonymous *wenian* by analogy with the *Heliand* 2817: *wennian mid willien*; but cf. *wēmað on willan*, *The Whale* 35, and see Note to line 36.

31. **geholena** was related by Grein to the verb *helan* ' to conceal '. The meaning indicated by the context, ' close friend ', was substantiated by Zupitza (*Archiv*, lxxxvi. 279), who pointed out another instance of the word in one of Ælfric's *Lives of the Saints* (No. 23, line 590, Thorpe's edition): *wē bēoð pīne geholan and ealne weg pīne midsprecan*; a second MS. reads *gehalan*, probably an ablaut variant and the same word as appears in a Wright-Wülker gloss (I, 18.18): *gehala vel gerūna, sinmistes vel consecretalis*. There appears to be little support for the Bosworth-Toller gloss ' protector '.

Constructions of the pattern *lȳt . . . geholena* are frequently to be found as examples of litotes in Old English poetry, and we are probably to take it that the exile has no one at all to confide in.

32. **warað.** To provide a subject for *warað* Boer emended *hine* to *hē*; but most editors have kept MS. *hine* and have taken *wræclāst* as the subject, although Miss Kershaw and Mossé have suggested that the real subject is ' thoughts ' understood. Used transitively *warian* usually means ' guard, hold, occupy '. Bosworth-Toller (*warian* IIIb) translate as ' take possession of ' and cite, as a parallel example of its use with a personal object, a passage from the *Heliand* 1001-3. Ekwall (*Anglia*

Beiblatt, xxxv. 134-5) translates the clause as ' exile falls to his lot ';
' exile claims him ', however, would retain the transitive form.

34. selesecgas. Like *seledrēorig* (25) this *sele-* compound is unique,
but unlike the former, *selesecgas* has been accepted as a compound by
most recent editors. Miss Kershaw justifies it by similar compounds
such as *seldguma* and *selepegn*. The contexts in which these occur in
Beowulf would indicate that they refer to retainers of a rather lowly
status, and *selesecgas* could have a similar meaning here; there is no
necessity to suppose that the exile intends a reference to his peers, for
the meaner retainers would be obvious contributors to the pleasures of
the hall he is recalling.

36. wenede tō wiste. The infinitive form *wenian* is found only in late
Old English prose; Klaeber in his glossary to *Beowulf*, and Holthausen,
prefer *wennan* on account of the cognate Germanic forms of this verb.
It is possible that in late Old English when the *-ode* preterite forms of class
II weak verbs were weakened to *-ede*, an analogical form *wenian* came
into use, facilitated by its similarity to the weak class II verb *wunian*.
Wenian has two distinct senses: ' accustom, train, fit ' and ' draw,
attract '. Bosworth-Toller point out that *wenian* followed by *tō* to
indicate completion of training is a frequent construction; cf. *wenian tō
gefeohte* (Ælfric's Homilies, edited by Skeat, II, XXV, line 571).
Thorpe's translation ' trained to the feast ' seems preferable, therefore,
to those which suggest that the wanderer's lord spoiled him. We are
not justified in assuming that his lord singled him out for special
attention, but rather that he accustomed the now exiled man to high
living, as he would all his young nobles; the contrast between then and
now is all the more telling because he has lost something which he had
taken for granted.

37 ff. The clause beginning *Forþon wāt sē . . .* has been held to be
incomplete because of the apparent lack of an object for *wāt*. Many
editors take the *ðonne* clause (39-40) to be in the same sentence and place
a semi-colon or stop after *gebindað* (40); but Imelmann (*Forschungen
zur Altenglischen Poesie*, p. 130), Miss Kershaw and Mossé begin a new
sentence with *ðonne*, including the *ðonne* clause with the lines which
follow it (41 ff.), a procedure which gives a better syntactical grouping,
for the *ðonne* clause explains the conditions under which the exile
pinceð him on mōde. But the problem of the object of *wāt* remains;
Miss Kershaw claims that this verb is repeated from line 29 and that its
object is to be inferred from the preceding passage, lines 30-36, although
this antecedent object is not made clear. Lines 34-6 cannot be relevant,
for these indicate what he remembers, not what he knows. Moreover,
since *forþon* is an adverb, as indicated by the inversion of subject and
verb which follow it, lines 37 ff. cannot be closely linked syntactically to
those which precede them; furthermore, there is a point in the MS. after

gedreas, which indicates a pause in the sense here. Sedgefield's claim that *wat* is used absolutely, meaning ' understands, has true knowledge ' is untenable because this use of *wāt* is found only after a comparative or along with a modifying adverb or adverbial phrase, for example in *ne ful gere wiste* (*Elene* 859) and *hī ne geara wistan* (*Psalm* 81.5); cf. Grein-Köhler, *witan* 5. Sieper and Wyatt suggest that there is anacoluthon here, which Wyatt claims is very effective. But an object for *wāt* is to be found within the framework of regular syntactical practice if lines 37-44 are taken as one sentence; it is then clear that what the exile knows is how, when he falls asleep (39-40), he dreams of his lord (41-4). The construction exemplifies the well-authenticated use of *wāt* introducing a clause without an explicit connecting word; cf. Bosworth-Toller, *witan* I (5) (a) and Grein-Köhler, *witan* 4. *Hū* (cf. lines 29-30) or perhaps *þæt*, is to be understood, for to put a conjunction before *pinceð* (41) would be misleading, because the *ðonne* clause is part of the larger clause after *wāt*, and to place it before *ðonne* would give an awkward juxtaposition of conjunctions; the poet therefore leaves it out as in the syntactically similar construction in *Vainglory* 77-80:

> Wite þē be þissum,
> gif þū ēaðmōdne eorl gemēte,
> þegn on þēode, þām bið simle
> gǣst gegæderad godes āgen bearn.

Here *þæt* is to be understood before *gif*.

38. lārcwidum is a compound found only once elsewhere, in *Andreas* 674, where the teacher is also of high rank, for *sōðfæstes* (673) probably refers to Christ. The custom of having young men trained by a famous man of noble rank was common; *v.* M. Rösler, *Englische Studien*, xlviii. 14-15. Cf. also Wealhðeow's injunction to Beowulf: *ond þyssum cnyhtum wes/lāra līðe* (1219-20).

longe, literally ' for a long time ', is an example of a typical Anglo-Saxon understatement; the implication is that the exile must for ever forgo his lord's advice. Cf. *lȳt . . . lēofra geholena* in line 31.

39. ðonne. Boer points out that the feelings of the *winelēas guma* are narrated in chronological order and supports this observation by noting that each section is introduced by *ðonne* (39, 45, 49, 51). He claims that this parallelism indicates clearly the correct punctuation of lines 39-40, and that in each section a new sentence is begun with *ðonne*. The parallelism is incomplete, however, for Boer ignores the word order. His claim is valid for lines 45 and 49, where *ðonne* is followed by inversion of subject and verb, indicating that it is to be taken adverbially and so begins a new sentence; but in lines 39 and 51 the verb is at the end of the clause, signifying subordination and the interpretation of *ðonne* as the conjunction ' when '.

40. earmne ānhogan. Cf. *earm ānhaga, Beowulf* 2368, and see Note on *ānhaga* in line 1.

41. þinceð. Ettmüller unnecessarily altered to *þynceð*; *i* for *y* is unusual in this text, but we have *mine* in line 27. The expression *þinceð him on mōde* appears to be a periphrasis for 'he dreams', an interpretation reinforced by the fact that falling asleep (39-40) precedes the wanderer's mental picture, whose unsubstantial nature is indicated by *þinceð*.

41b-44. The significance of this ceremony was made clear by Larson (*American Historical Review*, xiii. 461) when he showed that it was closely related to a Norwegian ceremony describing the initiation of a follower into the king's entourage, in *Norges Gamle Love* (edited Keyser and Munch, 1848), II, pp. 422 f. After kneeling, touching the hilt of the king's sword and kissing his hand, the candidate rose and took the oath of fealty. Kneeling a second time, he placed his folded hands between those of the king and kissed his new lord. It is this latter part of the ceremony only which our passage resembles. It may be, as Larson claims, that sword-touching was not required of all who entered the royal service, or it may be that the exile in his dream is not thinking of his initiation into the *comitatus*, but of one of the periodical distributions of treasure, at which a ceremonial demonstration of loyalty and affection was the retainer's response to his lord's generosity. That the latter is more probable is indicated by the *swā* clause linking the 'enjoyment' of the gift-throne with the ceremony, and by *Maxims* I, 67-68, in which not only are *hond* and *hēafod* linked with the *gifstōl* as here, but also the nature of the function, namely the distribution of treasure, is made explicit, as it is not in the *Wanderer* passage:

Hond sceal hēofod inwyrcan,   hord in strēonum bīdan,
Gifstōl gegierwed stondan,   hwonne hine guman gedǣlen.

Cf. also Ashdown's reference (*MLR*, xxii. 313) to a passage in *Olafs Saga Helga* from the *Heimskringla*, where Thorkel Amundarson *lagði hǫfuð sitt í kné jarli Thorfin* and asked for his protection, whereupon Thorfin bound Thorkel into his service. The laying of the head on the lord's knee is also mentioned in the *Bragða-Ölvis Rímur*, where it evidently symbolised the placing of the retainer's life into the lord's hands. A number of Icelandic sagas testify both to the stereotyped nature of this ceremonious action and to the considerable emotion which it evoked: *Þorsteins Saga Hvíta* (*Íslenzk Fornrit*, XI, p. 17); *Vápnfirðinga Saga* (*Íslenzk Fornrit*, XI, pp. 52 f.); *Víglundar Saga* (*Íslenzk Fornrit*, XIV, pp. 115 f.); in the following the homage is made to a lady and appears like a courtly parody of the ceremony in *The Wanderer: Þórðar Saga Hreðu* (*Íslenzk Fornrit*, XIV, p. 188). The editor is indebted to Dr. R. N. Ringler for drawing his attention to these passages. The laying of the hand on the lord's knee, normally to touch the sword laid there, is mentioned in Saxo Grammaticus, vii, 254. Since it was usual for gifts of value to be given at the initiation ceremony, it seems possible that the original oath of fealty might have been revived in this ceremony whenever treasure of value was distributed.

42. lecge. The MS. form is *lecge*, not *læge* as Wülker believed; a number of later editors have, in consequence, emended unnecessarily.

43. swā. . . . There appears to be some ellipsis here, *swā* being used with both adverbial force meaning ' just as ' (cf. Bosworth-Toller IV (1)(a)) and with the force of a temporal conjunction ' when ' (cf. Bosworth-Toller V(8)); cf. *Andreas* 926-7:

> Nō ðū swā swīðe synne gefremedest
> swā ðū in Achaia ondsæc dydest.

As Miss Grubl notes (*Studien zu den angelsächsischen Elegien*, p. 24) *hwīlum* in this clause refers to more than one occasion, and the reference to a repeated ceremony tells against interpretation as an initiation ceremony.

44. giefstōlas brēac. Conscious that *brūcan* generally takes the genitive, Thorpe and other early editors emend MS. *giefstōlas* to *giefstōles*. Grein keeps the MS. reading, taking it as an accusative plural; but Klaeber (*Anglia Beiblatt*, xvii. 300) points out that in at least two of the three examples of the accusative in Old English poetry, in the Psalms, Latin influence is probably responsible. There are, moreover, nearly a hundred examples of *brūcan* with the genitive in Old English poetry. Since the outcast is talking here of one lord, one *giefstōl* would be appropriate. The MS. form can in fact be taken as the expected genitive singular, for the *-as* ending occurs occasionally in late West-Saxon MSS.; cf. *Beowulf* 63, 2453, 2921 and Sievers-Brunner § 237, Anmerkung 1.

46a. Holthausen (*Anglia Beiblatt*, xxxii. 81) reads *him biforan gesihð* for metrical reasons; but the half-line may be read as type B with resolution of the second lift. Although a type B first half-line generally has alliteration on the first lift, alliteration on the second lift is occasionally found, as in *Beowulf* 3056.

46b. fealwe wēgas. Gollancz reads *wegas* and translates as ' the fallow ways '; but a long *e*, the regular development of *ǣ* in Non-West-Saxon (cf. Sievers-Brunner § 62, Anmerkung 2) is preferable here, both on account of the context and the stereotyped use of *fealu* with *wǣg*, as in *fealewe wǣgas* (*Andreas* 1589) and *fealone wǣg* (*The Gifts of Men* 53).

47. brēdan feþra. The plural *feþra* can mean wings, as in *Genesis* 1471. The birds may be spreading their wings or simply spreading their feathers for the purpose of preening them, as Miss Kershaw suggests, and as seems likely from the fact that they are bathing also.

48. Sweet's normalisation to *hægle* is unnecessary as *a* in place of the expected *æ* from fronting is not infrequent, by analogy with *a* in the plural forms where retraction has taken place before vowels in the inflexional endings; cf. Sievers-Brunner § 50, Anm. 6.

50. **sāre** has been variously interpreted: as the instrumental of a noun, by Grein-Wülker, Gollancz and Krapp-Dobbie; as an adverb, by Grein-Köhler; and as a nominative plural adjective agreeing with *benne*, by Miss Kershaw. This last interpretation appears to be the most idiomatic after the substantive verb; cf. *Genesis* 425, 1593, 2216. Moreover *sār* and *benn* are to be found closely linked in the compound *sārbennum* (*Andreas* 1239, *Guthlac* 1019). Taken as an adjective, *sāre* is anticipated and emphasised by *þȳ hefigran*.

æfter swǣsne. The accusative after *æfter* is rare, but is found where the idea of striving towards a goal is implied; cf. *Judith* 64-5, *Solomon and Saturn* 404. Here the wounds of his heart are grievous out of longing for the beloved man, the lord in line 41, about whom he has been dreaming.

50b-55. The syntactical problems in this much-discussed passage concern the relationship to the context of *sorg bið genīwad* (50), *grēteð glīwstafum* (52), *secga geseldan* (53), and *flēotendra ferð* (54). The solutions to the last three depend to some extent on interpretations put upon individual words, but the first may be solved on syntactical grounds alone. The position of *geondhweorfeð*, at the end of line 51, indicates that the *þonne* clause to which it belongs is subordinate. As such it is unlikely to depend on the verbs in line 52, for these, lacking a subject, do not constitute a complete clause. It is probable, therefore, that the *þonne* clause is dependent on *bið genīwad*.

51. **geondhweorfeð.** The prefix *geond-* gives an exhaustive sense to the simple verb, as in *geondscēawað* (52), *geondþence* (60) and *geondþenceð* (89); cf. also Grein-Köhler, *geond-*.

52. Since **grēteð** and **geondscēawað** appear to have no expressed subject, 'he' is often taken as the understood subject, an initial assumption which causes syntactical difficulties later in the passage; but an immediate objection is that the nearest antecedent would be *winelēas guma* (45), seven lines away and separated from the verbs by other nouns in the nominative. The object is usually taken to be 'them', referring to *māga* (51), which depends in the genitive on *gemynd*. Closer and less ambiguous subject and object are to be found if *grēteð* and *geondscēawað* are taken as parallel to *geondhweorfeð* (51) and as sharing with it *gemynd* as subject and *mōd* as object, the interpretation of lines 51 and 52 being ' . . . when recollection of kinsmen pervades his imagination, comes to it (the imagination) joyously, eagerly surveys it '.

glīwstafum. Mrs. Salmon (*MLR*, lv. 1-10) disputes the commonly held interpretation ' joyously, joyfully ', claiming that *glēo* means

' music ' as well as ' joy ' in Old English, and that *stæf* has many associations with magic practices; she would translate the word ' with magic
songs '. But this compound is of a widely attested pattern, in which
-stæf is habitually used as an abstract noun suffix, particularly with
nouns indicative of emotion; cf. *æfter sorgstafum* (*Juliana* 660), *sārstafum*
(*Guthlac* 234), *hearmstafas* (*Guthlac* 229), *gyrnstafa* (*Juliana* 245),
ārstafum preceded by prepositions in *Beowulf* 317, 382, 458, and an
exact syntactical parallel, *ārstafum* ' kindly ', with the dative plural
used adverbially, in *Riddle* 26. 24.

53. **secga geseldan.** *Geseldan* may be taken as the object, either
singular or plural, of *geondscēawað*, or as the subject of *swimmað*. The
phrase is often translated as ' companions/comrades of warriors/heroes ',
referring to the *māga* of line 51, who appear to the exile as spirits.
Suggestions that the phrase denotes living beings, who are occupants of
other ships (by Sedgefield) or sailors in a port where the exile is staying
(by Owen, *MLN*, lxv. 161-5) are at variance with the utter loneliness of
the exile, which is the theme of the passage. Midgley's suggestion that
the phrase refers to seagulls (*RES*, x. 53-4) has two drawbacks: in the
first place, gulls are not habitual companions of men; in the second
place, much of the force of his argument rests on an acceptance of the
parallelism of the phrase with *flēotendra ferð* and of the interpretation of
ferð as ' troop, crowd ', an unsupported meaning in Old English. Miss
Wardale's suggestion of an inanimate referent ' memories ' (*Chapters on
Old English Literature*, p. 41) has the merit of avoiding the pointless
redundancy of the equation of the companions of men with men. The
validity of this kind of solution is upheld by a similar use of *geselda* in
Riddle 80.3: *cyninges geselda*, which refers to a ' horn '. If we look for a
specific referent, of which *secga geseldan* is a variant, the closest and most
apt is *mōd*; first the hallucinatory vision of his kin penetrates his
imagination (51), greets it joyously, then eagerly surveys the ' companion
of men ', i.e. *mōd*, his imagination. Although one may not agree with
Mrs. Salmon's interpretation of *secga geseldan* as guardian spirits (*MLR*,
lv. 9-10), she provides a striking parallel construction from Old Icelandic,
where the *hugir* or free-ranging souls are described as companions of men,
fylgjar manna. The concept of a man's spirit or imagination as a separ-
able entity is to be found in the following lines (55-7) and is elaborated in
The Seafarer 58-62, concerning which see notes to these lines in Mrs.
Gordon's edition of the poem.

53b-54a. Modern editors take *swimmað* in a figurative sense, usually
with reference to phantoms of the exile's friends; cf. ' melt away ', by
Miss Kershaw and Krapp-Dobbie. Owen points out that this use is not
listed in OED before the sixteenth century. He maintains that even if
such a sense could be imposed on *swimman*, the meaning required for
onweg cannot be substantiated in Old English; it is OED's *away*, sense

5, ' into extinction, to nothing ', which first appears in 1340. If *swimmað ... onweg* is not associated with phantoms, however, his objection to the meaning of *onweg* is not valid, whether *swimmað* be taken literally or figuratively. Brewer (*MLN*, lxvii. 398) maintains that the figurative usage postulated for *swimmað* is a very common one, especially in poetry, and that paucity of records in Old English should prevent us from being too dogmatic. Owen's rejection of metaphorical meanings leads him to two major emendations, of *flēotendra* to *flēotende* ' ship ', and of *swimmað* to *swimmeð*.

The retention of MS. *oft* is preferable to the frequent emendation to *eft*; it emphasises that the dream-like state described is a recurrent one, as is also made clear by *swīpe geneahhe* (56); cf. the use of *oft* in line 40.

If *secga geseldan* is taken as a variant of *mōd* (51), then *flēotendra ferð* is the most probable subject for *swimmað*; since *ferð* can be neuter as well as masculine, the form can be taken as neuter plural. One meaning which has commonly been assigned to *ferð* in this context is spirit in the sense ' ghost, phantom ', although it has been doubted whether such a meaning is possible in Old English; cf. Ekwall, *Anglia Beiblatt*, xxxv. 135. *Ferð* has also been taken to mean ' host, crowd '; this meaning was first suggested by Boer, with emendation to *ferd*, and has latterly been put forward by Smithers (*English and Germanic Studies*, iv. 84), who takes *ferð* as an Old Norse poetic loanword, a supposition which requires, as he recognises, a much later date for the poem than is generally accepted. There is, however, no good reason for rejecting the usual meaning of the word in Old English, ' spirit ' in the sense ' soul, imagination ', although in consequence it seems probable that we must also accept the meaning ' of seafarers ' for the much-discussed *flēotendra*. Owen suggests that the evidence for this meaning is ' at best only less unsatisfactory than for " floaters in the air " and the like '. But although *flēotend* does not occur elsewhere in Old English, there is a strong parallel from *līpan* for the derivation of agent nouns from the present participle; just as we have *līpend* beside *lida*, we may have *flēotend* beside *flota*. The paucity of occurrences of *flota* beside *lida* suggests that *līpan* was a more popular verb for such derivation and would also account for the rarity of *flēotend*. But there are parallels for *ad hoc* uses of present participles as agent nouns; cf. the unique occurrence of *rōwend* ' sailor ' in *Andreas* 473 and the apparently extempore *drincendra drēam* used of men at a feast in *The Fortunes of Men* 79.

The effect of the whole clause is to give a parenthetic explanation of the strange illusions described in lines 50-53a, which can overtake a lonely suffering man at sea: ' the spirits of seafarers often swim away ', an explanation similar to that in *The Seafarer* 59-60: *mīn mōdsefa ... ofer hwæles ēpel hweorfeð wīde*. The detachment of mind from body is also envisaged and developed at some length in *The Metres of Boethius* XXIV.

54. bringeð. The subject of this verb is not independently expressed but, as with *grēteð* and *geondscēawað* (52), it is *māga gemynd* (51), the instigator of all the actions indicated by the four verbs in the clause, action which is resumed after the parenthetic remark of lines 53b-54a.

55. cūðra cwidegiedda. Midgley's interpretation of this phrase as ' articulate speech ', in contrast to mere noise (*RES*, x. 53-4), probably reads too much into *cūðra*. The use of this adjective suggests that what the exile misses is familiar speech from the lips of friends; cf. *Andreas* 198-9: *Ne synt mē winas cūðe,/ eorlas elpēodige*. Although *gied* can mean ' song ' or ' speech ' in Old English, the presence of *cwide-* as a first element, as of *word-* in *wordgyd* in *Beowulf* 3172, suggests that speech is referred to here. The element *giedd* is added probably because of the poetic convention that a formal utterance in a poem is ' sung '; cf. *gyd* in *Beowulf* 2154.

The words *nō ðǣr fela* in the preceding line are characteristic of Old English litotes and indicate the disappointment of the exile as he realises that the figures before him are mirages, because they are completely silent.

The whole passage (50-55) may be translated literally:

> Sorrow is renewed when the recollection of kinsmen pervades his imagination, joyously comes to, eagerly surveys the companion of men (i.e. his imagination)—the spirits of seafarers often swim away —but it (the recollection) brings no familiar utterances there at all.

58-9. These lines have been held to indicate the sadness of the wanderer when he contemplates the transience of life; cf. Mrs. Gordon (*RES*, v. 6) and Cross (*Neophilologus*, xlv. 67). The wanderer may or may not be sad; his references to his own sorrows and his own state of mind hitherto have been to the past, although we may assume that his generalisation on the fate of exile wanderers, which are loosely linked to lines 58 ff. by means of *Forðon* ' therefore ', indicate a melancholy state of mind. It is not, however, sadness which is in question here, but his mind ' growing dark '. The force of *gesweorcan* has probably been underestimated; *swearc* in *Guthlac* 1052 clearly indicates deep sorrow, and with the prefix *ge-* the sense of *gesweorce* (59) is likely to be ' despair '. The verb *gesweorcan* clearly implies a change of state, but the subjunctive form *gesweorce* in the indirect question clause in line 59 leaves open the question whether the wanderer's *mōdsefa* ' mind ' *does* or *might well* ' become dark '. The case for the mind of the wanderer actually becoming dark can only be firmly maintained if the phrase *geond ðās woruld* is put inside the subordinate *for hwan* clause, as in Mrs. Gordon's translation ' Therefore I can think of no reason in this world why my heart should not grow dark . . . '. But the phrase *geond* *þās woruld* is closely linked with the verb *geþencan*, to which it gives an exhaustive sense similar to that of the prefix *geond-*, and also confines discussion of the wanderer's state of mind to the evidence of this world alone. *Þās*, moreover, is strongly emphasised, since it carries the alliteration; cf. the same combination of this phrase with *geþencan* in *Christ and Satan* 642, where this function is made explicit:

> Uton, lā, geþencan   geond þās worulde,
> þæt wē hǣlende   hēran onginnan.

This exhortation occurs between a description of the fate of the souls doomed eternally to hell during Christ's harrowing of hell and a picture of the joys of heaven, the whole purpose of the passage being to point the contrast between this world and the other worlds of heaven and hell. The sense of *geþencan* in *The Wanderer* is either ' to form an idea in the mind ' (sense VI in Toller, under which he lists this line), or ' to perceive after consideration, learn ' (Toller, sense VIII). Either of these inter-pretations can be supported, partly by the dependence upon *geþencan* of the indirect interrogative clause which follows, and partly by the presence in the *þonne* clause of *geondþence*, which emphasises the per-fective aspect of *geþencan*, for *geþencan* embodies the conclusions drawn from the survey of the mortality of men indicated by *geondþence*. There is an echo of the outlook of these lines in lines 88-9; but there the ' wise man ' has his observations confined to this life which he accepts as dark, whereas the wanderer here is not so confined.

59. Grein's emendation of MS. *mod sefan minne* to *mōdsefa mīn ne* has generally been accepted, since *gesweorce* not only requires a subject but, being intransitive, cannot take an accusative. A scribal error of *sefan* for *sefa* is readily attributable to the influence of *sefan* (57) in the immediately preceding MS. line, or possibly it is a scribal emendation of *sefa* as a result of the erroneous belief that it was followed by the masculine accusative singular of *mīn*, instead of *mīn* in the nominative and the negative particle *ne*. On the other hand, final added nasals are occasionally to be found in *The Exeter Book*; cf. *ēadwelan* (*The Phoenix* 251).

60. **eal geondþence.** *Eal* may be taken as an adjective qualifying *līf*, or as an adverb, since it occurs in the same half-line as *geondþence*; cf. *Andreas* 1146: *eall formeltan*, 1590: *grund eall forswealg*, and see the glossary to K. R. Brooks' edition of *Andreas*.

61. **flet ofgēafon** is a periphrastic phrase for ' they died '; cf. *woruld ofgeaf*, *Genesis* 1164 etc., *Beowulf* 1681, and *feorh ofgēfon*, *The Fates of the Apostles* 12. *Flet*, literally ' floor ', comes by synecdoche to mean ' hall ', as in *Beowulf* 1949, 2017.

62. **mōdge maguþegnas.** The idea of youthfulness often present in *magu* is not always present in the compound, meaning ' retainer '; for example, it is used of Æschere, Hrōðgar's veteran counsellor, in *Beowulf*

1405. The whole phrase occurs as a stereotype in *Andreas* 1140, 1515, *Menologium* 82, *Beowulf* 2757 (in the singular).

62b-63. The *swā* clause is made subordinate and the *hū* clause taken as parenthetic by Miss Kershaw; but *swā* as a conjunction meaning ' just as ' depends awkwardly upon the *ponne* clause. We obtain a smoother sequence of ideas if *swā* begins a new sentence; the sudden death of men becomes the subject of the wanderer's reflections: ' Thus this world day by day decays and falls away '. The particular reflection in lines 61-62a prompts the general one in lines 62b-63.

64. wearpan. Many editors, including Krapp-Dobbie and Mossé, emend to *weorpan*. But *ea* for *eo* is common in Northumbrian texts and not infrequent in Kentish; cf. also *beorn* for *bearn* in *Beowulf* 1880. Confusion between the two diphthongs was frequent at all periods in Northumbrian, common in the Vespasian Psalter, and sporadic in late West-Saxon (cf. Sievers-Brunner § 35, and Anm. 1).

65. woruldrīce indicates the kingdom of this world in contrast to the kingdom of heaven. Most of the occurrences of the compound in Old English are in specifically Christian poems such as *Genesis*, *Christ*, *Juliana* and *Elene*, and also in the homilies. Although it is the speaker's concern to emphasise the futility of this world, the very use of the word *woruldrīce* implies a conscious contrast with the eternal world.

65b, 66a. In both lines *bēon* or *wesan* is to be understood after *sceal*, as frequently in Old English; cf. Bosworth-Toller, *sculan* III.

66b. hrædwyrde ' hasty of speech ' does not appear to occur elsewhere, but there are other compounds of *-wyrde,* which is cognate with *word;* cf. *wærwyrde* ' careful in speech ', *Precepts* 57, and *fægerwyrde, Precepts* 12. The same idea is expressed in *The Fortunes of Men* 50: *bið ǣr his worda tō hræd.*

69. gielpes tō georn. Gollancz claims that there has been an erasure of two letters in the MS. after *georn,* but examination of the MS. fails to reveal any sign of erasure. A distinction has probably to be made between *gielp* meaning ' glory, renown ' and the later homiletic use of the word where the meaning has degenerated to ' over-bearing arrogance '; cf. Lindheim, *RES,* xxv. 193. The injunctions to caution and moderation in one's desire for *gielp* in this passage suggest that it is a legitimate aspiration.

72. hrepra gehygd. The genitive plural *hrepra* with the singular *gehygd* may be a poetic use, as suggested by Wyatt and Mossé; on the other hand, the cognate Gothic form *hairpra* is found only in the plural. The phrase *purh hrepra gehygd* occurs in *Beowulf* 2045. Klaeber (*Anglia,* xxxv. 470) points to the phrases *brēost gehygdum* and *mōd gehygdum* in *Beowulf* which have a similar meaning, and suggests that the conception may be modelled on biblical phraseology, e.g. *Matthew* 9.4.: *quid cogitatis mala in cordibus vestris ?*

73. gǣstlic is a rare adjective in Old English and usually means ' spiritual ', like the much more common *gāstlic*. But such a meaning is not appropriate to this context and *gǣstlic* here is probably the Old English form of modern *ghastly*, with the meaning ' terrible ', or ' awesome ' as suggested by Smithers (*Medium Ævum*, xxvi. 141). It is to be taken as a cognate of OE *gǣstan* ' to seek to terrify ' (cf. *Juliana* 17) and Gothic *usgáisjan* ' to terrify ', and thus a homonym of *gǣstlic* ' spiritual ' rather than a variant sense of that word.

74. eall þisse worulde wela. The MS. *ealle* has been emended to *ealre* to agree with *worulde* by Grein-Wülker and a number of other editors; yet others have followed Ettmüller in emending to *eall* to agree with *wela*. The latter is to be preferred, for there is evidence from similar contexts of *eall* referring to the wealth rather than to the world; cf. Alfred's translation of Boethius (Sedgefield's edition), p. 28, lines 8-9: *eall þises middaneardes wela*, p. 27, lines 19-20: *ealra ðissa woruldǣhta and welena*, and the Blickling Homilies, p. 51, line 30: *eal eorðan wela*. Scribal error in the addition of *e* to *eall* is readily understandable owing to the presence of final *e* in both the preceding and the two following words; on the other hand the scribe may have written *ealle* in anticipation of a plural *welan*, as in the Old English translation of *Luke* 16.9: *þisse worulde welan* which translates the Vulgate *mamona*.

75. This line is echoed closely by *The Gifts of Men* 28: *missenlīce geond þisne middangeard* and *The Fortunes of Men* 64-5: *Swā missenlīce . . . geond eorþan scēat*.

76. biwāune. Many have followed Ettmüller in emending unnecessarily to *biwāwne*. Krapp-Dobbie keep *biwāune*, pointing out that the full plural form of the past participle of *biwāwan* would be *biwāwene*; the disappearance of *e* in the medial, open, lightly stressed syllable resulted in the vocalisation of *w* to *u* when followed by a consonant, giving the form *biwāune*.

77. hrȳðge. Bosworth-Toller suggested ' dismantled ', ' ruinous ', as the meaning of this unique adjective, as if it were cognate with Old Icelandic *hrjóða* ' to strip, clear '; alternatively they proposed ' tottering ', taking the adjective as cognate with OE *hriðian* ' to shake, have a fever '; but OE *hriðian*, *hrið* and their cognates in Gothic and Old High German are all restricted to fever. Moreover, the form *hrȳðge* must be from earlier *hrȳðige*, and the disappearance of the short medial vowel of the adjectival ending presupposes long *ȳ* in the stem; cf. Sievers-Brunner § 159b. Strunk (*MLN*, xviii. 72), was the first to point out the possible connection of *hrȳðge* (with a long vowel) and *hrīð* (102), which occurs in a similar context and is also a unique form in Old English, although almost certainly cognate with ON *hríð* ' storm ', especially ' snowstorm '. A closer cognate, however, pointed out by Mrs. Gordon, is ON *hryðja*, a feminine noun meaning ' rough weather, tempest '.

ederas. Usually listed under the back-mutated form *eodor*, this noun is cognate with ON *iaðarr*, OHG *etar*, and OS *edar*, with the basic meaning ' border, enclosure '. In the stereotyped phrase *in under eodoras/ederas* in *Beowulf* 1037, *Genesis* 2447, 2489, the meaning appears to have been transferred by synecdoche from the enclosure to include the thing enclosed, the house or hall, so that the meaning ' precincts ' is appropriate as here; cf. also the use of the word in *The Laws of Ethelbert*, 29. This development would be similar to that of *tūn* in OE and ON.

78. **wōriað** literally means ' wander ', but there are a number of figurative uses in Old English. Bosworth-Toller's ' totter (are ruinous) ' does not bring out the continuity of the decay suggested in the similar context in *The Ruin* 12, for which ' moulder ' is suggested; cf. also Bessinger, p. 78, *wōrian* ' roll in pieces, crumble '.

waldend licgað. Marquardt (*Die Altenglischen Kenningar*, p. 154) points out that *waldend* by itself refers to God as a rule, and that an attributive word is to be understood here in order to complete the kenning *winsæles waldend*, i.e. the retainers assembled there; but it is not uncommon for the attributive word to remain unexpressed if the same word is used earlier in the sentence, as it is here.

79. **drēame bidrorene.** Deprivation of joy is a common element in elegiac motifs in Old English poetry; cf. the same phrase in *Guthlac* 626, *drēamum bidrorene* in *Guthlac* 901 and *drēame bedæled* in *Beowulf* 1275.

80a. **wlonc bī wealle.** Lawrence (*JGP*, iv. 476) suggests that the phrase can hardly be taken literally to mean that all the men met their death beside the wall, and that *bī wealle* belongs rather with *wlonc* than with *gecrong*, so that the reference is to the place where they were proud in the days when they inhabited the now ruined halls. But, however the next three lines are interpreted, there is no difficulty about taking the direct meaning, namely that the men all fell beside the wall, so that their fate is associated with the fate of their buildings and the warriors are thought of as perishing in defence of their city.

80b-84. The opening phrase, *Sume wīg fornōm*, opens a similar passage in *Elene* 131; cf. also *Hildebrand* 43: *inan wīc furnam* and *Beowulf* 1080: *Wīg ealle fornam*. Much of the discussion of this passage derives from the relationship assumed between *sume* and the *sumne* phrases; there are three of the latter, which are held by Bright to indicate individual deaths referred to collectively by *sume* (80). According to Wülker (*Grundriss zur Geschichte der Angelsächsischen Litteratur*, p. 206), all four references are of equal status; few, however, would now agree that the *sumne* phrases refer to death at sea, in the hunt and through illness or old age. These phrases, dealing with the disposal of individual bodies, are most naturally taken as distributive of *sume*, the number of men struck down in war; if they were taken as parallel to *sume*, then the *sumne* phrase (83), which refers to burial, would not be of the same kind as the other three; it is preferable to take it, along with the other *sumne* phrases, as one of the ways in which the bodies of the fallen may be disposed of. *Sume* may well be an understatement for ' not a few '; cf. *Beowulf* 1113.

81b-82a. Thorpe's suggestion that *fugel* is a poetic term for ship, more recently put forward again by Krapp-Dobbie, has the disadvantage that no other figurative uses of this kind elsewhere in Old English literature can be cited in support. One obvious difficulty of the bird interpretation is that no bird could carry off a corpse; but if, as seems likely (see Cross ' On *The Wanderer* lines 80-84 ', pp. 92-3), the bird's action symbolises the distribution of a corpse across the world, there would be no difficulty to the medieval mind; cf. Wyatt's reference to the mythical bird carrying off a man, on the Celtic stone at Meigle, and the eagle which carries off Chaucer in *The House of Fame*. An actual bird would of course remove a body piecemeal, although the result would be the same; the bird is probably one of the ' birds of battle ' of Old English poetry, namely the raven or the eagle. The carrying away of the body across the sea suggests that the bird is the sea-eagle, the usual carrion eagle in Old English poetry; for its colouring see *The Battle of Brunanburh* 62-3 and for its habitat, *The Seafarer* 23, 25.

82b-83a. **gedǣlan** has a number of meanings, one being ' divide up ', so that *dēaðe gedǣlde* may mean ' dismembered at death '. On the other hand it may mean ' give as a share ' (*Beowulf* 71) or ' get as a share ' (*Genesis* 296); the latter meaning would be appropriate here, the two half-lines being translated: ' the wolf got one as his share at the death '. In either case the wolf takes his place alongside the bird in his traditional role of battle scavenger.

83b. **drēorighlēor** is a unique compound, although other adjectives of a similar type are to be found; cf. especially *tēarighlēor* (*Genesis* 2276) and *drēorigmōd* (*Genesis* 2805). This sad-faced man who buries one of the slain appears to be in a position similar to that of the last survivor in *Beowulf*, the *ān æfter eallum* who *unblīðe hwearf* (2268) *giōmormōd*, and who buried the treasures of his tribe after *Ealle hīe dēað fornam* (2236), the one who alone survived (2237-8) to mourn his friends, *winegeōmor* (2239).

85. **Ȳpde.** Many editors emended to this form an alleged MS. reading *ypðe*; but, as Mackie first noted, the MS. reading is *ypde*, and no emendation is necessary.

eardgeard occurs only once elsewhere, with reference to Jerusalem in *Christ* 55. There are no grounds for extending its meaning to the whole world; *þisne eardgeard* is the land or city whose fate the wanderer has just been describing.

86. **burgwara** has been taken as the genitive plural of *burgware*

'citizens', depending on *breahtma*; cf. Gollancz's translation 'deprived of the noise of its inhabitants'. It has also been taken as nominative plural with the meaning 'cities, communities' by Wyatt and Krapp-Dobbie; but it is doubtful if *burgware* can be identified with the buildings of a city apart from the community who live in them. Moreover, the whole point of line 87 is that the buildings are empty because they are devoid of their inhabitants; *burgwara* is best taken therefore as genitive plural and as meaning 'inhabitants'. Instead of being dependent on *burgwara*, *breahtma* may be parallel to it with asyndetic parataxis; the translation would then be 'until, deprived of its inhabitants, its sounds . . .'

87. **enta geweorc.** Examples of this formula and of minor variants such as *enta ǣrgeweorc* are frequently found applied to many objects belonging to an older civilisation, but particularly to buildings as here, in *The Ruin* 2, *Maxims* II, 2, and *Beowulf* 2717. The identical half-line, *eald enta geweorc*, occurs in *Andreas* 1495, where it refers to pillars which are *storme bedrifene* (see edition by K. R. Brooks, p. 113) like the ruins in *The Wanderer* 77; in *Beowulf* 2774 it is used of an ancient barrow.

88. **wealsteal** does not occur elsewhere, although a similar compound *burgsteall*, also unique, appears in *The Ruin* 28. This compound refers to the place where the walls stand, which is described in the preceding passage, lines 73-87.

wīse geþōhte 'considered wisely, pondered over'; cf. *Psalm* 118. 59b: *wīse þence*, which translates Latin *cogitavi*.

89. **geondþenceð** is probably an echo of *geþencan geond* (58) and *geondþence* (60) as noted by Greenfield (*JEGP*, 1. 461). It echoes the latter more particularly, for the life of man is the subject of consideration of both line 60 and line 89.

90. **frōd in ferðe.** *Frōd* does more than echo *wīse* (88). It usually refers to the wisdom of the old, and so the speaker is 'wise from experience'; cf. *frōd on fyrhðe* (*Elene* 463) and, with the accusative *frōdne*, in *Elene* 1163.

feor is an adverb of time here as in *Beowulf* 1701: *feor eal gemon* and *Elene* 1141: *feor ǣr beforan*.

91. **ond þās word ācwið** is a stereotyped introduction to a speech; cf. *Beowulf* 2046: *ond þæt word ācwyð* and *Judith* 283: *ond þæt word ācwæð*.

92-3. The use of *Hwǣr cwōm* rather than *Hwǣr bið* for most of the questions does not exclude these from dependence on the widespread Christian Latin *ubi sunt* motif (cf. Cross, ' " Ubi Sunt " Passages in Old English—Sources and Relationships', *Vetenskaps-Societetens i Lund, Årsbok*, 1956, pp. 25-44), for *abierunt* is occasionally found in place of *sunt* in Latin versions of the formula, and in Old English translations we have *cwōm* and *cwōmon*; cf. Vercelli Homily X: *Hwǣr cōman middangeardes gestrēon? Hwǣr cōm worulde wela? Hwǣr cwōm foldan fǣgernes? Hwǣr cōman þā þe geornlicost ǣhta tiledon ond ōþrum eft yrfe lǣfdon?* Cf. also Blickling Homily VIII and *Christ and Satan* 36: *Hwǣr cōm engla ðrym?*

93. Hwǣr cwōm symbla gesetu ? A singular verb with plural subject is not infrequently found in Old English poetry, especially when the predicate precedes the subject; see Stoelke's study of incongruence in Old English, p. 17. A desire for rhetorical balance may well have contributed to the use of *cwōm*, in conformity with the three singular forms in the preceding line.

94-5. A similar but longer list of vanished joys introduced by *Ēalā* occurs in *Christ and Satan* 163-7; cf. especially *Ēalā drihtenes þrym* with *Ēalā þēodnes þrym* (95).

95. Hū sēo þrāg gewāt. Cf. *Genesis* 135: *sēo tīd gewāt . . . sceacan* and *Genesis* 1420-1: *rīmgetæl rēðre þrāge/daga forð gewāt.* In *Beowulf* 2883 *sīo þrāg* means ' time of hardship or distress '; here it is probably the opposite, ' the good old days ', as suggested by K. R. Brooks (*Andreas and the Fates of the Apostles*, p. 103).

97. on lāste accompanied by the dative of the person, here *lēofre duguþe*, is a frequent construction in Old English poetry. The phrase means literally ' in the track of ' and may be used with the connotation of time, as in *Genesis* 945, or of place, as in *The Phoenix* 440. Both are probably intended in *Genesis* 86-7: *him on lāste setl,/ . . . wīde stōdan*, in which the fallen angels have left behind them their thrones in heaven, as in *The Wanderer* passage, to which it is syntactically parallel. The poet is harking back to the theme of lines 75-87; the only vestige of the dead warriors is the wall of their hall, beside which they fell.

98. wyrmlīcum fāh. In the unique compound *wyrmlīcum* the second element *līc* must be the noun meaning ' body, form ', as in the *Beowulf* compounds *eoforlīc* (303) and *swīnlīc* (1453), which denote boar figures worked in relief on helmets. By analogy with these, *wyrm* is likely to be the word for serpent. French suggests (*MLN*, lxvii. 526) that the phrase refers to the channels made in the outer wood of wall timbers by beetle larvae. The wall referred to, however, is likely to be a stone one; cf. note on *eald enta geweorc* (87). Bowen has suggested (*Explicator*, xiii (1955), Item 26) that the reference here may be to maggot patterns on Neolithic stone monoliths; but it seems unlikely that the poet, aiming for precision where possible—like most Anglo-Saxon writers, would use *weal* for such an object when *stapol* was available. The phrase would appropriately describe a serpentine motif, possibly in the form of a frieze, carved in relief, and the effect of light and shadow produced by the relief would account for the use of *fāh* ' variegated '. Serpents and serpentine sea beasts were favourite decorative motifs in Roman stone bas-reliefs and friezes, particularly in Western Europe;

cf. the illustrations in *Recueil Général des Bas-Reliefs, Statues et Bustes de la Gaule Romaine* by Émile Espérandieu (Paris, 1907-55), I, p. 97; III, p. 360; IV, pp. 236, 247, 283, 285, 411; VI, pp. 380, 420, 455; VII, p. 104.

99. **fornōman.** The frequent emendation of the ending to *-on* is unnecessary, as *-an* occurs as a preterite plural ending of strong verbs in Kentish and Northumbrian; cf. Sievers-Brunner § 364.2 and Campbell § 735(e).

100. **wyrd sēo mǣre.** The inverted word-order here indicates some emphasis, probably the personification of *wyrd* ' fate '. In similar phrases with normal word order, in *Genesis* 1399: *þæt is mǣro wyrd*, and *Elene* 1063: *þā mǣran wyrd*, ' event(s) ' is indicated by the context as the meaning for *wyrd*.

101. **þās stānhleoþu** probably denotes the stone walls of buildings, the storm-swept *ederas* of line 77; cf. the similar reference to buildings in *under stānhliðum* in *Daniel* 61.

102. **hrið** is a unique form in Old English, but probably cognate with ON *hríð* ' tempest, storm ' (but in early writers only ' snowstorm '), *v. An Icelandic English Dictionary* by R. Cleasby and G. Vígfusson and Note to *hrȳðge* (77).

hrūsan is Thorpe's emendation of MS. *hruse* to make the form the object of *bindeð*. The fact that the object precedes its verb may have led to an error in copying. Grein takes *hrūse* as an accusative of a strong form of the noun, but the numerous other occurrences of this noun provide no evidence to support such an assumption.

103a. **wōma** is nominative in apposition to *hrīð*. Etymologically it is cognate with ON *ómun* ' voice ' and Latin *vox*; cf. also *Ómi* ' Voice of the wind ', a name of Odin. The word has oracular connotations in Old English, suggesting something strange and secret in the passages where it is linked with a dream: *Daniel* 110, 538 and *Elene* 71; *v.* Marquardt, pp. 180-1 and P. O. E. Gradon, *Cynewulf's Elene*, p. 26. *Wōma* refers clearly to noise in *Elene* 19 and *Exodus* 100, and in the compound *heofonwoma* in *Christ* 834, 998; cf. also *wōm and wōp* in *Christ and Satan* 332, and *hildewōma* in *Andreas* 218. But in the compounds *dægredwōma* and *dægwōma* ' harbinger of day ' there is no question of sound, and a semantic shift is evident from voice or noise announcing something to the act of announcement itself. The power of the phrase *wintres wōma* lies in the linking of both aspects of meaning.

103b. The clause *þonne won cymeð* is often taken as parenthetic, e.g. by Krapp-Dobbie; but it is more closely linked in sense with the following lines than with those which precede it, and it is syntactically linked with the principal clause *nīpeð nihtscūa* by reason of the inversion of subject and predicate in the latter. A semi-colon therefore appears preferable to a comma after *wōma*.

104. Cf. *The Seafarer* 31-2 and *Beowulf* 547. *Nihtscūa* is the subject of both *nīpeð* and *onsendeð*: ' the shadow of night grows black and drives from the north a fierce hailstorm '; for *onsendan* in a similar physical context cf. *Judgement Day*, I, 53-4: *leohtes weard/ofer ealne foldan fæþm fȳr onsendeð*.

105. **hrēo hæglfare** ' a fierce hailstorm '. *Hæglfare* is a unique compound, but an analogous formation is *wolcenfaru* in *Daniel* 378 and *wolcnfare* in *Riddle* 3.71.

hæleþum on andan ' to the vexation of men '. *On andan*, with the dative of the person to whom annoyance or vexation is caused, occurs several times in Old English poetry; cf. *Elene* 969, *Beowulf* 708, 2314 and *on ondan* in *Guthlac* 773.

106. Miss Kershaw takes *Eall* to qualify *rīce* in the nominative: ' all the realm of earth is full of tribulation '. But *earfoðlic* means rather ' difficult, grievous '; cf. the adverbial use in *Andreas* 514-15: *ūs . . . earfoðlīce/gesǣleð* ' it goes hard with us ' (*v.* Brooks' edition, p. 139). It is preferable therefore to take *rīce* as in an oblique case and translate: ' all is fraught with hardship in the kingdom of the world '. *Eorþan rīce* echoes *þās woruld* (58), *þisse worulde* (74) and *þisne middangeard* (75), and is probably in conscious contrast to the *ēcan rīce* and *heofonlīcan rīce* of the homilists, as in Blickling Homily III (EETS edition, p. 31).

107. **wyrda gesceaft** occurs once elsewhere in Old English, in *Daniel* 132; the meaning in both is probably ' ordered course of events ' (Toller, *gesceaft* II, 5). Similar phrases occur in other Christian poems: *wyrda bigang* (*Elene* 1123), *wyrda gangum* (*Elene* 1255), *wyrda geryno* (*Elene* 589, 812, *Daniel* 149). God is described elsewhere as the ruler of events, *wyrda waldend* (*Andreas* 1056, *Elene* 80), and as not subject to *wyrda* in *Maxims* I, 8-9: *God ūs ēce biþ/ne wendaþ hine wyrda*. Man's powerlessness is indicated in *Resignation* 117-18: *þonne mon him sylf ne mæg/wyrd onwendan, þæt he þonne wel þolige*. Lines 106 and 107 imply that the idea of change in *onwendeð* is for the worse; cf. *The Ruin* 25. Erzgräber suggests the possibility of a conscious link with line 85, where God is described as *ælda Scyppend* (*loc. cit.* pp. 72-3); certainly the picture of all creation subject to decay (106-7) indicates the subordination of creation to the creator who has instituted decay (85).

108-9. The resemblance of these two lines to stanzas 76 and 77 of the Old Norse collection of precepts, the *Hávamál*, was first pointed out by R. M. Meyer in *Die altgermanische Poesie nach ihren formelhaften Elementen beschrieben* (Berlin, 1889), p. 321. The lines, repeated in both stanzas, are

> Deyr fé, deyja frændr,
> deyr sjálfr it sama.

The order and enumeration are the same as in *The Wanderer*: property, friends, oneself. Our poem has, in addition, *mǣg*; but since Old Norse *frǽndr* denotes both friends and relatives, two words in Old English are needed to cover the same area of meaning. Miss Kershaw (p. 167) notices the repetition of the first of these two lines in strophe 21 of the *Hákonarmál*, where the following line, translated ' desert grows every hill and dale ', is similar in sentiment to line 110 of *The Wanderer*. But these three lines differ from those in the Old Norse texts in being set in a Christian homiletic mould, with *hēr* referring to this world and *lǽne* expressing a viewpoint congenial not only to the homilists but also to the poet Cynewulf, as in *Elene* 1269-70: [*feoh*] *ǽghwām bið/lǽne under lyfte*, a passage which occurs in the elegiac epilogue which bears his signature. Cf. the Old English translation of Boethius (Sedgefield's edition, p. 130, lines 30-1): *þās lǽnan þing bīoð tō metanne wið ðā ēcan; v.* Erzgräber, *loc. cit.* pp. 73-4. The concept of everything in the world as being on loan, and hence transitory, is behind the use of *lǽne*, which is cognate with OE *lǽn* ' loan '.

110. **gesteal** occurs only once elsewhere in Old English, in Cockayne's *Leechdoms* iii, p. 102, line 27: *þan tōþa þā tunga tō spǽce gesteal ys.* Toller translates doubtfully as ' apparatus '; but cf. the cognate OHG *gestell* ' framework ', a meaning which gives good sense in the poem.

111b. The closest Old English parallel to the construction here is *Andreas* 1161: *Gesǣton searuþancle sundor tō rūne.* The difference between *tō rūne* here and elsewhere, and *æt rūne* in *The Wanderer* may be that between ' council ' and ' consultation '; cf. ON *heita einn at rúnum* ' to consult '. That the wanderer is communing with himself is indicated by the reflexive *him;* that his reflections are inward is suggested by *on mōde*, and that his meditations are private is indicated by *sundor.*

112-14a. **torn** may mean ' anger ' or ' grief '; since the tenor of much of the poem is the keeping of one's troubles to oneself, the latter is the most probable meaning here. Mrs. Gordon (' Traditional Themes in the Old English *Wanderer* and *Seafarer* ', p. 3) points out an analogue to this passage in the Rule of St. Columba, where an anchorite is warned against talking with one who grumbles about what he is not able to remedy, and Erzgräber (*loc. cit.* pp. 79-81) has pointed out parallels in Boethius, Book II, Metr. 8 and Book IV, Pr. 7.

114b-115. The *ār* and *frōfor* of God are also to be found in association with each other in *Beowulf* 1272-3: *him tō Anwaldan āre gelȳfde,/ frōfre ond fultum;* cf. also *The Metres of Boethius* i. 78-9.

The preposition *tō* here means ' from, at the hands of ', marking the source from which something is sought; cf. Bosworth-Toller *tō* (5h).

The use here of *fæstnung* as an abstract noun is unique in Old English; but, as Miss S. I. Tucker (*Essays in Criticism* viii. 237) points out, *eal sēo fæstnung* is a phrase of multiple meaning and depth, and *fæstnung* has many references: stability (as here), fortification, ratification and covenant, all these ideas being full of Biblical overtones.

Erzgräber has pointed to a similar use of Latin *stabilitas* (*loc. cit.* pp. 76-7) in Boethius, Book IV, Pr. 6: *ex diuinae mentis stabilitate sortitur.* Although the Old English translation of Boethius does not render the noun by *fæstnung*, there is in the same chapter nevertheless—the chapter containing the celebrated illustration of the wheel of fortune—the sentence

> þēah þā mǣtestan ealle hiora lufe wenden
> tō þisse worulde, hī ne magon þǣron wunigan,
> ne tō nāuthe ne weorðað, gif hī be nānum dǣle
> ne bēoð gefæstnode tō Gode.

GLOSSARY

The Glossary is intended to include all occurrences of all forms in the text. The order of words is strictly alphabetical; æ follows **ad**, þ and ð are treated as one letter and follow **t**, words prefixed by **ge-** follow **gearwe**. The gender of nouns is indicated by the abbreviations *m.*, *f.*, *n.* (*noun* is implied). The numbers after *sv.* and *wv.* refer to the classes of strong and weak verbs respectively, as indicated in A. Campbell's *Old English Grammar*. The line references to emended forms are italicised.

ācweðan *sv.* 5 to utter; 3 *sg. pres.* **ācwið** 91.

ācyþan *wv.* 1 to make known 113.

æfter *prep. w. acc.* (longing) for 50.

ælde *m. pl.* men; *gen.* **ælda** 85.

ǣr *adv.* formerly 43, beforehand 113; *conj.* before 64, 69.

æsc *m.* spear; *gen. pl.* **asca** 99.

æt *prep. w. dat.* in 111.

ætgædre *adv.* together 39.

āh *v.* I possess; 3 *sg. pres. subj.* **āge** 64.

āna *adj.* alone; *wk. nom. sg. m.* 8.

anda *m.* vexation; *dat. sg.* **andan** 105.

ānhaga *m.* solitary one; *nom. sg.* 1.

ānhoga *m.* solitary one; *acc. sg.* **ānhogan** 40.

ār *f.* mercy; *acc. sg.* **āre** 1, 114.

ārǣdan *wv.* 2 to determine; *pp.* **ārǣd** 5.

asca *see* **æsc**.

āsecgan *wv.* 3 to confess 11.

baþian *wv.* 2 to bathe 47.

benn *f.* wound; *nom. pl.* **benne** 49.

beorht *adj.* bright; *voc. sg. f.* 94.

boorn *m.* man; *nom. sg.* 70, 113.

bēot *n.* vow; *acc. sg.* 70.

bēoð *see* **wesan**.

bī *prep. w. dat.* beside 80.

bidǣlan *wv.* 1 to deprive; *pp. nom. sg. m.* **bidǣled** 20.

bidrēosan *sv.* 2 to deprive; *pp. nom. pl. m.* **bidrorene** 79.

biforan *prep. w. dat.* in front of 46.

bihrēosan *sv.* 2 to cover; *pp. nom. pl. m.* **bihrorene** 77.

bihrorene *see* **bihrēosan**.

bindan *sv.* 3 to bind; 3 *sg. pres.* **bindeð** 102; 3 *pl. pres.* **bindað** 18; 3 *sg. pres. subj.* **binde** 13.

bið *see* **wesan**.

biwāune *see* **biwāwan**.

biwāwan *sv.* 7 to blow upon; *pp. nom. pl. m.* **biwāune** 76.

biwrēon *sv.* 1 to cover; 3 *sg. pret.* **biwrāh** 23.

biwrāh *see* **biwrēon**.

blǣd *m.* glory; *nom. sg.* 33.

bōt *f.* remedy; *acc. sg.* **bōte** 113.

brǣdan *wv.* 1 to spread 47.

brēac *see* **brūcan**.

breahtm *m.* revelry; *gen. pl.* **breahtma** 86.

91

brēost *n.* breast; *dat. pl.* **brēostum** 113.

brēostcofa *m.* heart; *dat. sg.* **brēostcofan** 18.

brimfugol *m.* sea-bird; *acc. pl.* **brimfuglas** 47.

bringan *wv.* 1 to bring; 3 *sg. pres.* **bringeð** 54.

brūcan *sv.* 2 to enjoy; 3 *sg. pret.* **brēac** 44.

brytta *m.* bestower; *acc. sg.* **bryttan** 25.

būne *f.* cup; *voc. sg.* 94.

burgware *m. pl.* inhabitants; *gen.* **burgwara** 86.

byrnwiga *m.* warrior; *voc. sg.* 94.

cann *v.* I know; 3 *sg. pres. subj.* **cunne** 69, 71, 113.

cearo *f.* sorrow; *nom. sg.* 55; *acc. sg.* **ceare** 9.

clyppan *wv.* 1 to embrace; 3 *sg. pres. subj.* **clyppe** 42.

cnēo *n.* knee; *acc. sg.* 42.

cnyssan *wv.* 1 to dash against; 3 *pl. pres.* **cnyssað** 101.

collenferð *adj.* resolute; *nom. sg. m.* 71.

cuman *sv.* 4 to come; 3 *sg. pres.* **cymeð** 103; 3 *sg. pret.* went **cwōm** 92 (3), 93.

cunne *see* **cann.**

cunnian *wv.* 2 to make trial of; 3 *sg. pres.* **cunnað** 29.

cūð *adj.* familiar; *gen. pl. n.* **cūðra** 55.

cwæð *see* **cweðan.**

cweðan *sv.* 5 to speak; 3 *sg. pret.* **cwæð** 6, 111.

cwic *adj.* alive; *gen. pl. m.* **cwicra** 9.

cwidegiedd *n.* utterance; *gen. pl.* **cwidegiedda** 55.

cwīþan *wv.* 1 to bewail 9.

cwōm *see* **cuman.**

cymeð *see* **cuman.**

cyssan *wv.* 1 to kiss; 3 *sg. pres. subj.* **cysse** 42.

dǽl *m.* portion; *acc. sg.* 65.

dearr *v.* I dare; 1 *sg. pres. subj.* **durre** 10.

dēað *m.* death; *dat. sg.* **dēaðe** 83.

dēope *adv.* deeply *89.*

deorc *adj.* dark; *wk. acc. sg. n.* **deorce** 89.

dōgor *n.* day; *gen. pl.* **dōgra** 63.

dōmgeorn *adj.* eager for glory; *nom. pl. m.* **dōmgeorne** 17.

drēam *m.* joy; *dat. sg.* **drēame** 79.

drēorig *adj.* sad; *acc. sg. m.* **drēorigne** 17.

drēorighlēor *adj.* sad-faced; *nom. sg. m.* 83.

drēosan *sv.* 2 to collapse; 3 *sg. pres.* **drēoseð** 63.

duguþ *f.* body of mature men; *nom. sg.* 79; *dat. sg.* **duguþe** 97.

durre *see* **dearr.**

eal(l) *adj.* all; *nom. sg. m.* **eall** 74; *nom. sg. f.* **eal** 79, 115; *nom. sg. n.* **eall** 106, **eal** 110; *gen. pl. n.* **ealra** 63.

eal *adv.* completely 36, 60.

ēalā *interj.* alas 94 (2), 95.

eald *adj.* old; *nom. pl. n.* 87.

eardgeard *m.* dwelling place; *acc. sg.* 85.

eardstapa *m.* wanderer; *nom. sg.* 6.

earfoð *n.* hardship; *gen. pl.* **earfeþa** 6.

earfoðlic *adj.* fraught with hardship; *nom. sg. n.* 106.

earm *adj.* wretched; *acc. sg. m.* **earmne** 40.

earmcearig *adj.* careworn; *nom. sg. m.* 20.

edor *m.* precinct; *nom. pl.* **ederas**
77.

eft *adv.* again 45.

ellen *n.* courage; *dat. sg.* **elne** 114.

elne *see* **ellen.**

ent *m.* giant; *gen. pl.* **enta** 87.

eorl *m.* man; *nom. sg.* 84, 114;
dat. sg. **eorle** 12; *acc. pl.* **eorlas**
99; *gen. pl.* **eorla** 60.

eorþe *f.* world; *gen. sg.* **eorþan** 106,
110.

eorðscræf *n.* grave; *dat. sg.*
eorðscræfe 84.

ēðel *m.* native land; *dat. sg.* **ēðle** 20.

fæder *m.* father; *dat. sg.* 115.

fægen *adj.* happy; *nom. sg. m.* 68.

færlīce *adv.* suddenly 61.

fæste *adv.* firmly 13, 18.

fæstnung *f.* stability; *nom. sg.* 115.

fāh *adj.* variegated; *nom. sg. m.* 98.

feallan *sv.* 7 to fall; 3 *sg. pres.*
fealleþ 63.

fealu *adj.* yellowish green; *acc. pl.*
m. **fealwe** 46.

fela *indeclinable pron. w. gen.* many
54.

feoh *n.* property; *nom. sg.* 108.

feohgīfre *adj.* avaricious; *nom. sg.*
m. 68.

feor *adv.* far 21, 26, 90.

ferian *wv.* 1 to carry; 3 *sg. pret.*
ferede 81.

ferð *n.* spirit; *nom. pl.* 54; *dat. sg.*
mind **ferðe** 90.

ferðloca *m.* breast; *nom. sg.* 33;
acc. sg. **ferðlocan** 13.

feter *f.* fetter; *dat. pl.* **feterum** 21.

feþer *f.* feather; *acc. pl.* **feþra** 47.

findan *sv.* 3 to find 26.

flēotan *sv.* 2 to float; *pres. p. gen.*
pl. m. **flēotendra** seafarers 54.

flēotendra *see* **flēotan.**

flet *n.* hall; *acc. sg.* 61.

folde *f.* earth; *gen. sg.* **foldan** 33.

for *prep. w. instr.* on account of 59.

forht *adj.* afraid; *nom. sg. m.* 68.

forniman *sv.* 4 to destroy; 3 *sg.*
pret. **fornōm** 80; 3 *pl. pret.*
fornōman 99.

fornōm, fornōman *see* **forniman.**

forþolian *wv.* 2 to forgo 38.

forþon *adv.* therefore 17, indeed 37,
58, 64.

forðweg *m.* way forth; *dat. sg.*
forðwege 81.

frēfran *wv.* 1 to comfort 28.

frēomæg *m.* noble kinsman; *dat. pl.*
frēomægum 21.

frēond *m.* friend; *nom. sg.* 108.

frēondlēas *adj.* friendless; *acc. sg.*
m. **frēondlēasne** 28.

frēorig *adj.* frozen; *nom. sg. m.* 33.

frōd *adj.* wise; *nom. sg. m.* 90.

frōfor *f.* solace; *acc. sg.* **frōfre** 115.

fugel *m.* bird; *nom. sg.* 81.

ful *adv.* completely 5.

gæstlic *adj.* terrible; *nom. sg. n.* 73.

geāra *adv.* long since 22.

geārdæg *m.* day gone by; *dat. pl.*
geārdagum 44.

geare *see* **gearwe.**

gearwe *adv.* clearly 71; **geare** 69.

gebīdan *sv.* 1 to wait 70; 3 *sg. pres.*
experiences **gebīdeð** 1.

gebind *n.* expanse; *acc. sg.* 24, 57.

gebindan *sv.* 3 to bind fast; 3 *pl.*
pres. **gebindað** 40.

gecringan *sv.* 3 to fall; 3 *sg. pret.*
gecrong 79.

gecrong *see* **gecringan.**

gedǣlan *wv.* 1 to get (as a share);
3 *sg. pret.* **gedǣlde** 83.

gedrēas *see* **gedrēosan.**

gedrēosan *sv.* 2 to perish; 3 *sg. pret.*
gedrēas 36.

gefēra m. companion; dat. sg. **gefēran** 30.

gefremman wv. 1 to afford 16, to act 114.

gehealdan sv. 7 to keep; 3 sg. pres. **gehealdeþ** 112.

gehola m. close friend; gen. pl. **geholena** 31.

gehwā pron. each; dat. sg. m. **gehwām** 63.

gehwylc pron. each; instr. sg. m. **gehwylce** 8.

gehȳdan wv. 1 to conceal; 3 sg. pret. **gehȳdde** 84.

gehygd f. thought; nom. sg. 72.

gemengan wv. 1 to mingle; pp. **gemenged** 48.

gemon v. I remember; 3 sg. pres. 34, 90.

gemynd n. recollection; nom. sg. 51.

gemyndig adj. mindful; nom. sg. m. 6.

genāp see **genīpan**.

geneahhe adv. frequently 56.

genīpan sv. 1 to grow dark; 3 sg. pret. **genāp** 96.

genīwian wv. 2 to renew; pp. **genīwad** 50, 55.

geoguð f. youth; dat. sg. **geoguðe** 35.

geond prep. w. acc. throughout 3, 58, 75.

geondhweorfan sv. 3 to pervade; 3 sg. pres. **geondhweorfeð** 51.

geondscēawian wv. 2 to survey; 3 sg. pres. **geondscēawað** 52.

geondþencan wv. 1 to meditate on; 1 sg. pres. **geondþence** 60; 3 sg. pres. **geondþenceð** 89.

georn adj. eager; nom. sg. m. 69.

georne adv. eagerly 52.

gesæt see **gesittan**.

gesceaft f. ordained course; nom. sg. 107.

geselda m. companion; acc. sg. **geseldan** 53.

gesēon sv. 5 to perceive; 3 sg. pres. **gesihð** 46.

geset n. dwelling; nom. pl. **gesetu** 93.

gesihð see **gesēon**.

gesittan sv. 5 to sit; 3 sg. pret. **gesæt** 111.

gesteal n. framework; nom. sg. 110.

gesweorcan sv. 3 to grow dark; 3 sg. pres. subj. **gesweorce** 59.

geþencan wv. 1 to perceive, consider 58; 3 sg. pret. **geþōhte** 88.

geþōhte see **geþencan**.

geþyldig adj. patient; nom. sg. m. 65.

gewāt see **gewītan**.

geweorc n. creation; nom. pl. 87.

gewītan sv. 1 to depart; 3 sg. pret. **gewāt** 95.

giefstōl m. throne; gen. sg. **giefstōlas** 44.

gielp m. glory; gen. sg. **gielpes** 69.

glēaw adj. wise; nom. sg. m. 73.

glīwstafum adv. joyfully 52.

gold n. gold; nom. sg. 32.

goldwine m. generous lord; nom. sg. 35; acc. sg. 22.

grētan wv. 1 to come to; 3 sg. pres. **grēteð** 52.

guma m. man; nom. sg. 45.

habban wv. 3 to have; 3 sg. pres. **hafað** 31.

hægl m. hail; instr. sg. **hagle** 48.

hæglfaru f. hailstorm; acc. sg. **hæglfare** 105.

hæle m. man; nom. sg. 73.

hæleþ m. man; dat. pl. **hæleþum** 105.

hafað see **habban**.

hagle see **hægl**.

hār *adj.* grey; *wk. nom. sg. m.*
  hāra 82.
hātheort *adj* impulsive; *nom. sg.*
  m. 66.
hē *pron.* 3 *sg. m.* he; *nom.* 2, 13, 14,
  34, 41, 43, 64, 69, 70, 113; *acc.*
  hine 32, 35; *gen.* his 13, 14, 35,
  37, 41, 112 (2), 113; *dat.* him 1
  (reflexive), 10, 31 (reflexive), 41
  (reflexive), 46, 111, 114 (reflexive).
hēafod *n.* head; *acc. sg.* 43.
hēah *adj.* high; *nom. sg. m.* 98;
  acc. sg. m. hēanne 82.
healdan *sv.* 7 to hold, keep; 3 *sg.*
  pres. subj. healde *14*.
hēan *adj.* wretched; *nom. sg. m.* 23.
hēanne *see* hēah.
hefig *adj.* heavy; *compar. wk. nom.*
  pl. f. hefigran 49.
help *f.* help; *acc. sg.* helpe 16.
hēo *pron.* 3 *sg. f.* it; *nom.* 96.
heofon *m.* heaven; *dat. pl.* heofonum 107, 115.
heolstor *m.* darkness; *dat. sg.*
  heolstre 23.
heorte *f.* heart; *gen. sg.* heortan 49.
hēr *adv.* here 108 (2), 109 (2).
hī *pron.* 3 *pl. m.* they; *nom.* 61;
  gen. hyra 18.
him *see* hē.
hine, his *see* hē.
holm *m.* sea; *acc. sg.* 82.
hond *f.* hand; *acc. pl.* honda 43;
  dat. pl. hondum 4.
hordcofa *m.* heart; *acc. sg.* hordcofan 14.
hrædwyrde *adj.* hasty of speech;
  nom. sg. m. 66.
hrēo *adj.* troubled; *nom. sg. m.* 16;
  fierce *acc. sg. f.* 105.
hrēosan *sv.* 2 to fall; 48; *pres. p.*
  nom. sg. f. hrēosende 102.
hrēran *wv.* 1 to stir 4.
hreþer *n.* mind; *gen. pl.* hreþra 72.

hrīm *m.* frost; *acc. sg.* 48; *instr. sg.*
  hrīme 77.
hrīmceald *adj.* icecold; *acc. sg. f.*
  hrīmcealde 4.
hrīð *f.* snowstorm; *nom. sg.* 102.
hrūse *f.* earth; *acc. sg.* hrūsan *102*;
  gen. sg. 23.
hryre *m.* fall; *dat. sg.* 7.
hrȳðig *adj.* exposed to storms;
  nom. pl. m. hrȳðge 77.
hū *adv.* how 95; *conj.* 30, 35, 61, 73.
hwǣr *adv.* where 92 (3), 93 (2);
  conj. 26.
hwæt *pron. n.* what; *instr. sg.*
  hwan 59.
hweorfan *sv.* 3 to go 72.
hwider *adv.* whither 72.
hwīlum *adv.* at times 43.
hycgan *wv.* 3 to think; 3 *sg. pres.*
  subj. hycge 14.
hyge *m.* mind; *nom. sg.* 16.
hyra *see* hī.

ic *pron.* 1 *sg. m.* I; *nom.* 8, 10, 11,
  19, 23, 26, 58, 60; *acc.* mec 28;
  dat. mē *27*.
īdel *adj.* desolate; *nom. sg. m.* 110;
  nom. pl. n. īdlu 87.
in *prep. w. dat.* in 12, 18, 27, 44, 65,
  81, 84, 90.
indryhten *adj.* very noble; *nom. sg.*
  m. 12.
is *see* wesan.
iū *adv.* formerly 22.

lǣne *adj.* transitory; *nom. sg. m.*
  108b, 109 (2); *nom. sg. n.* 108a.
lagulād *f.* seaway; *acc. pl.* lagulāde
  3.
lārcwide *m.* counsel; *dat. pl.*
  lārcwidum 38.

lāst *m.* track; *dat. sg.* lāste 97.

lēas *adj.* destitute; *nom. pl. f.* lēase 86.

lecgan *wv.* 1 to lay; 3 *sg. pres. subj.* lecge 42.

lēof *adj.* dear; *gen. sg. m.* lēofes 38; *dat. sg. f.* lēofre 97; *gen. pl. m.* lēofra 31.

licgan *sv.* 5 to lie; 3 *pl. pres.* licgað 78.

līf *n.* life; *acc. sg.* 89; *acc. pl.* 60.

longe *adv.* for a long time 3, 38.

lȳt *indeclinable w. partitive gen.* small number 31.

mæg *v.* I can; 1 *sg. pres.* 58; 3 *sg. pres.* 15, 64; 1 *sg. pret.* meahte 26.

mǣg *m.* kinsman; *nom. sg.* 109; *gen. pl.* māga 51.

mǣre *adj.* famous; *nom. sg. f.* 100.

māga *see* mǣg.

mago *m.* youth; *nom. sg.* 92.

maguþegn *m.* retainer; *nom. pl.* maguþegnas 62.

maþþumgyfa *m.* giver of treasure; *nom. sg.* 92.

mē *see* ic.

meahte *see* mæg.

mearg *m.* steed; *nom. sg.* 92.

mec *see* ic.

meoduheall *f.* meadhall; *dat. sg.* meoduhealle 27.

metud *m.* lord; *gen. sg.* metudes 2.

mid *prep. w. dat.* by means of 4, 29, 114.

middangeard *m.* world; *nom. sg.* 62; *acc. sg.* 75.

milts *f.* mercy; *acc. sg.* miltse 2.

mine *m.* affection; *acc. sg.* 27.

mīn *adj.* my; *nom. sg. m. 59*; *acc. sg. m.* minne 10, 19, *22*; *acc. sg. f.* mīne 9.

missenlīce *adv.* in various places 75.

mōd *n.* heart, mind, spirit; *acc. sg.* 51; *dat. sg.* mōde 41, 111.

mōdcearig *adj.* troubled in heart; *nom. sg. m.* 2.

mōdig *adj.* noble; *nom. pl. m.* mōdge 62.

mōdsefa *m.* heart, soul; *nom. sg.* 59; *acc. sg.* mōdsefan 10, 19.

mon *m.* man; *nom. sg.* 109.

mondryhten *m.* liege lord; *acc. sg.* 41.

nǣfre *adv.* never 69, 112.

nāles *adv.* not at all 32; nāllæs 33.

nān *pron. w. partitive gen.* no one; *nom. sg. m.* 9.

ne *adv.* not 15, 16, 58, *59*, 64, 66 (2), 67 (2), 68 (3), 69, 112.

nēah *adv.* near 26.

nemþe *conj.* unless 113.

nihthelm *m.* shadow of night; *acc. sg.* 96.

nihtscūa *m.* shade of night; *nom. sg.* 104.

nīpan *sv.* 1 to grow black; 3 *sg. pres.* nīpeð 104.

nis *see* wesan.

nō *adv.* not at all 54, 66, 96.

norþan *adv.* from the north 104.

nū *adv.* now 9, 75, 97.

of *prep. w. dat.* from 113.

ofer *prep. w. acc.* across 24, 57, 82.

ofgiefan *sv.* 5 to abandon; 3 *pl. pret.* ofgēafon 61.

oft *adv.* often 1, 8, 17, 20, 40, 53, 90.

on *prep. w. dat.* on 42, 97; in 35, 41, 105, 111, 115.

ond *conj.* and; 23, 34, 39, 42 (2), 43, 48, 63, 89, 91, 101.

ongietan *sv.* 5 to understand 73.

onsendan *wv.* 1 to drive; 3 *sg. pres.*
  onsendeð 104.
onwæcnan *wv.* 1 to awaken; 3 *sg.*
  pres. **onwæcneð** 45.
onweg *adv.* away 53.
onwendan *wv.* 1 to change; 3 *sg.*
  pres. **onwendeð** 107.
oþberan *sv.* 4 to carry off; 3 *sg. pret.*
  oþbær 81.
oþþæt *conj.* until 71, 86.
oþþe *conj.* or 26, 28.

rīce *n.* kingdom; *dat. sg.* 106.
rūn *f.* (secret) meditation; *dat. sg.*
  rūne 111.
rycene *adv.* quickly 112.

sǣ *f.* sea; *acc. sg.* 4.
sǣlan *wv.* 1 to fasten 21.
sār *adj.* sore; *nom. pl. f.* **sāre** 50.
sceal *v.* I have to; 3 *sg. pres.* 37, 56,
  65, 66, 70, 73, 112; 3 *sg. pret.*
  sceolde 3, 8, 19.
sceolde *see* **sceal**.
scyppend *m.* creator; *nom. sg.* 85.
sē *pron.* he; *nom. sg. m.* 29, 37, 112;
  he who 88; *acc. sg. m.* **þone** 27;
  dat. sg. m. **þām** 31, 56, 114; *adj.*
  that; *nom. sg. m.* 16, 82.
sēcan *wv.* 1 to seek; 3 *sg. pres.*
  sēceð 114; 1 *sg. pret.* **sōhte** 25.
secg *m.* man; *gen. pl.* **secga** 53.
sefa *m.* heart; *acc. sg.* **sefan** 57.
seledrēam *m.* joy in the hall; *nom.*
  pl. **seledrēamas** 93.
seledrēorig *adj.* sad at the loss of
  the hall; *nom. sg. m.* 25.
selesecg *m.* hall retainer; *acc. pl.*
  selesecgas 34.
sendan *wv.* 1 to send 56.
sēo *adj. f.* that; *nom. sg.* 95, 100,
  115; *acc. sg.* **þā** 113.
sinc *n.* treasure; *gen. sg.* **sinces** 25.

sincþege *f.* receiving of treasure;
  acc. sg. 34.
sindon *see* **wesan**.
siþþan *conj.* since 22.
slǣp *m.* sleep; *nom. sg.* 39.
slīþen *adj.* cruel; *nom. sg. f.* 30.
snāw *m.* snow; *acc. sg.* 48.
snottor *adj.* wise; *nom. sg. m.* 111.
sōhte *see* **sēcan**.
somod *adv.* together 39.
sorg *f.* anxiety, sorrow; *nom. sg.*
  30, 39, 50.
sōþe *adv.* truly 11.
sprecan *sv.* 5 to utter; 3 *sg. pres.*
  spriceð 70.
stānhleoþu *see* **stānhliþ**.
stānhliþ *n.* stone wall; *acc. pl.*
  stānhleoþu 101.
stōdon *see* **stondan**.
stondan *sv.* 6 to stand; 3 *sg. pres.*
  stondeð 74, 97, 115; 3 *pl. pres.*
  stondaþ 76; 3 *pl. pret.* **stōdon** 87.
storm *m.* storm; *nom. pl.* **stormas**
  101.
sum *pron.* a certain one; *acc.*
  sg. m. **sumne** 81, 82, 83; *acc.*
  pl. m. **sume** 80.
sundor *adv.* apart 111.
swā *adv.* so 6, 19, 62, 75, 85, 111;
  conj. as 14, 43, as if 96.
swǣs *adj.* beloved; *acc. sg. m.*
  swǣsne 50.
sweotule *adv.* openly 11.
swimman *sv.* 3 to swim; 3 *pl. pres.*
  swimmað 53.
swīþe *adv.* very 56.
symbel *n.* feast; *gen. pl.* **symbla** 93.

til *adj.* good; *nom. sg. m.* 112.
tō *prep. w. dat.* to 36; as 30; from
  115; *adv.* too 11, 66 (2), 67 (2),
  68 (3), 69, 112.
torn *n.* grief; *acc. sg.* 112.
trēow *f.* faith; *acc. sg.* **trēowe** 112.

þā *adj.* that, those; *acc. sg. f.* 113 (see **sēo**); *nom. pl. m.* 77; *nom. pl. n.* 78.

þǣr *adv.* there 54; *conj.* where 115.

þæt *pron.* it, that; *instr. sg. n.* **þȳ** 49; *conj.* that 12, 13, 41.

þām *see* **sē**.

þās *see* **þes**.

þe *rel. pron. indeclinable* who 27, 29, 31, 37, 56, 112, 114; to whom 10.

þēahþe *conj.* although 2.

þēaw *m.* custom; *nom. sg.* 12.

þēoden *m.* prince; *gen. sg.* **þēodnes** 95.

þes *dem. adj.* this; *nom. sg. m.* 62; *acc. sg. m.* **þisne** 75, 85, 88; *acc. sg. f.* **þās** 58; *gen. sg. f.* **þisse** 74; *nom. sg. n.* **þis** 110; *acc. sg. n.* 89; *acc. pl. n.* **þās** 91, 101.

þincan *wv.* 1 to seem; *3 sg. pres.* **þinceð** 41.

þis, þisne, þisse *see* **þes**.

þonan *adv.* thence 23.

þone *see* **sē**.

þonne *adv.* then 45, 49, 88, 103; *conj.* when 39, 51, 60, 70, 74.

þrāg *f.* time; *nom. sg.* 95.

þrym *m.* glory; *voc. sg.* 95.

þrȳþ *f.* might; *nom. pl.* **þrȳþe** 99.

þȳ *see* **þæt**.

ūhta *m.* hour before dawn; *gen. pl.* **ūhtna** 8.

under *prep. w. acc.* beneath (of extent) 96; *w. dat.* beneath (of place) 107.

ūs *see* **wē**.

wāc *adj.* lacking in moral strength; *nom. sg. m.* 67.

wadan *sv.* 6 to travel 5; *1 sg. pret.* **wōd** 24.

wælgīfre *adj.* greedy for slaughter; *nom. pl. n.* **wælgīfru** 100.

wælsleaht *m.* slaughter; *gen. pl.* **wælsleahta** 7, 91.

wǣpen *n.* weapon; *nom. pl.* 100.

wēre *see* **wesan**.

waldend *m.* ruler; *nom. pl.* 78.

wanhȳdig *adj.* reckless; *nom. sg. m.* 67.

warian *wv.* 2 to claim; *3 sg. pres.* **wara**ð 32.

wāt *v.* I know; *1 sg. pres.* 11; *3 sg. pres.* 29, 37; *3 sg. pret. subj.* felt **wisse** 27.

waþem *m.* wave; *gen. pl.* **waþema** 24, 57.

wē *pron.* 1 *pl.* we; *dat. m.* **ūs** 115.

weal *m.* wall; *nom. sg.* 98; *dat. sg.* **wealle** 80; *nom. pl.* **weallas** 76.

wealsteal *m.* wall foundation; *acc. sg.* 88.

wearþan *sv.* 3 to become 64; *3 sg. pres.* **weorþeð** 110.

wēg *m.* wave; *acc. pl.* **wēgas** 46.

wel *adv.* well 114.

wela *m.* wealth; *nom. sg.* 74.

wēman *wv.* 1 to entice 29.

wenian *wv.* 1 to accustom; *3 sg. pret.* **wenede** 36.

weorþeð *see* **wearþan**.

weoruld *see* **woruld**.

wer *m.* man; *nom. sg.* 64.

wērig *adj.* tired; *acc. sg. m.* **wērigne** 57.

wērigmōd *adj.* weary at heart; *nom. sg. m.* 15.

wesan *v.* to be ; *3 sg. pres.* **bið** 5, 12, 30, 50, 55, 73, 108 (2), 109 (2), 112, 114; **is** 106; **nis** 9; *3 pl. pres.* **bēoð** 49; **sindon** 93; *3 sg. pret. subj.* **wēre** 96.

wēste *adj.* deserted; *nom. sg. m.* 74.

wīg *n.* war; *nom. sg.* 80.

wiga *m.* warrior; *nom. sg.* 67.

willan *v.* to wish; 3 *sg. pres.* **wille**
72; 3 *sg. pres. subj.* 14; 3 *sg.*
pret. subj. **wolde** 28.

wind *m.* wind; *dat. sg.* **winde** 76.

winedryhten *m.* dear lord; *gen. sg.*
winedryhtnes 37.

wineléas *adj.* friendless; *nom. sg.*
n̄i. 45.

winemǣg *m.* loyal kinsman; *gen.*
pl. **winemǣga** 7.

winsǣl *n.* winehall; *nom. pl.*
winsalo 78.

winter *m.* winter; *gen. sg.* **wintres**
103; *gen. pl.* **wintra** 65.

wintercearig *adj.* desolate as winter;
nom. sg. m. 24.

wis *adj.* wise; *nom. sg. m.* 64.

wise *adv.* wisely 88.

wisse *see* **wāt.**

wist *f.* feast; *dat. sg.* **wiste** 36.

wita *m.* wise man; *nom. sg.* 65.

wiðstondan *sv.* 6 to withstand 15.

wlonc *adj.* proud; *nom. sg. f.* 80.

wōd *see* **wadan.**

wolde *see* **willan.**

wōma *m.* harbinger; *nom. sg.* 103.

won *adj.* dark; *nom. sg. m.* 103.

word *n.* word; *acc. pl.* 91.

wōrian *wv.* 2 to moulder; 3 *pl. pres.*
wōriað 78.

worn *m.* large number; *acc. sg.* 91.

woruld *f.* world; *acc. sg.* 58;
weoruld 107; *gen. sg.* **worulde** 74.

woruldrīce *n.* realm of the world;
dat. sg. 65.

wrǣclāst *m.* path of exile; *nom. sg.*
32; *acc. pl.* **wrǣclāstas** 5.

wrāþ *adj.* fierce; *gen. pl. m.*
wrāþra 7.

wulf *m.* wolf; *nom. sg.* 82.

wunden *sv.* 3 *pp.* twisted 32.

wundrum *adv.* wonderfully 98.

wyn *f.* (object of) joy; *nom. sg.* 36;
dat. pl. **wynnum** 29.

wyrd *f.* course of events; *nom. sg.* 5,
100; *dat. sg.* **wyrde** 15; *gen. pl.*
wyrda 107.

wyrmlīc *n.* serpent shape; *dat. pl.*
wyrmlīcum 98.

ȳpan *wv.* 1 to destroy; 3 *sg. pret.*
ȳpde 85.